The Mystery Which Is Christ in You

"The Hope of Glory"

(Colossians 1:27)

Book I of the Barnabas Series

Cho Larson

Albertville, AL

Published by Warner House Press of Albertville, Alabama USA

Copyright © 2022 Cho Larson
Cover Design and Illustration © 2022 Ian Loudon, OKAY Media
Interior Design © 2022 Warner House Press

All rights reserved. No part of this book may be used or reproduced in any manner whatsoever without written permission, except in the case of brief quotations in critical articles and reviews. For more information, contact

Warner House Press
1325 Lane Switch Road
Albertville, Alabama 35951
USA

Published 2022
Printed in the United States of America

Cover image used under license from Shutterstock.com.

Unless otherwise noted, all scripture quotations are taken from HOLY BIBLE, NEW INTERNATIONAL VERSION®. Copyright © 1973, 1978, 1984 by International Bible Society. Used by permission of Zondervan Publishing House.

Scripture quotations marked ESV are from The Holy Bible, English Standard Version®, Copyright © 2001 by Crossway Bibles, a publishing ministry of Good News Publishers. Used by permission. All rights reserved.

Scripture quotations marked NKJV are from the New King James Version®. Copyright © 1982 by Thomas Nelson. Used by permission. All rights reserved.

Scripture quotations marked NLT are from the Holy Bible, New Living Translation, Copyright © 1996, 2004, 2007, 2013, 2015 by Tyndale House Foundation. Used by permission of Tyndale House Publishers Inc., Carol Stream, Illinois 60188. All rights reserved.

26 25 24 23 2 3 4 5

ISBN: 978-1-951890-35-3

Dedicated to:

Robert & Gayle DeGroot whose godly lives inspire me.

"As for you, see that what you have heard from the beginning remains in you. If it does, you also will remain in the Son and in the Father. And this is what he promised us—eternal life."

(1 John 2:24–25)

Table of Contents

Prepare to Sleuth	ix
1: Preparations of a Bride	1
2: One in Christ	11
3: Confidence and Assurance	21
4: A Foundation from the Beginning	29
5: Created for Fellowship	37
6: United in our Gatherings	47
7: Partakers of the Bread of Life	57
8: Games We Play with Darkness	65
9: Wandering from Home	75
10: Dressed and Ready	83
11: A Joyful Bride	91
12: March Forward in the Light	99
13: Overcomers in Christ	109
14: Assurance in Christ	121
15: Double Portions	129
16: The Revelation of Yeshua, our Lord and Savior	139
17: Kept Safe to the End	151
Cherishing Found Treasure	161
Acknowledgments	165

Prepare to Sleuth

The Mystery Which is Christ in You is the first book of the Barnabas series. Barnabas ministered in the early church as a preacher and is a great model for us. He served in keeping with the meaning of his name: "Son of Encouragement." That is the purpose of this book: to encourage Jesus' followers to search out the mystery of Christ's indwelling presence and grow in grace and knowledge. This is a practical, life-applicable trek through the Bible to search out the clues to this great truth.

What does it mean to be "in Christ?" Can anyone completely define the union we have with our Savior? This study book proclaims a Gospel that is very simple, yet a great mystery. By faith and in the waters of baptism we are made one with our Lord and Savior. We know how we are made one with Christ. We understand the promise of Christ returning for us and then our dwelling with Him in heaven forever, but what does it mean in everyday life?

This study does not present a three-step program for living as one with the Father, Son, and Holy Spirit. Instead, the learner is shown the path for a life-long journey of faith and eternal hope. Open your Bible with one hand, this study guide with the other, and let's begin to explore the mysteries of this miraculous Good News.

It's a challenge to illustrate the reality of being in Christ and Him Indwelling us. We might offer an example like: if a child fell into a batch of creamy milk chocolate, she would be in the chocolate and the chocolate would be in her. But this example falls short because her whole being is not totally permeated with chocolate.

When the sailors threw Jonah overboard in the middle of a raging storm, we might say that Jonah was in the sea and the sea was in him. But the saltwater Jonah gulped down only churned in his stomach and didn't penetrate to his heart and soul. A more accurate example of oneness is when he finally obeyed God and marched off, his head wrapped with seaweed, to deliver the Lord's message to the people of Nineveh.

A father-and-son relationship offers us a better example. Jim Sr. and Jimmy Jr. are the spitting image of each other. Little Jimmy tries to walk like his dad, talk like his dad, and wear his hat just like his dad. Jim's genes are in Jimmy and it's obvious in the mischievous twinkle in his eyes, and even in the way he laughs. But this example falls apart when Jimmy turns into a teenager and wants to be his own person. He gets angry when dad tries to parent him.

In reality, there is nothing in this material, temporal world that perfectly illustrates what it means to be in Christ. The image on the title page offers a good visual. We are the wick saturated in the oil of the Spirit and burning brightly in the power of the Spirit. Like the wick, we don't lose our unique identity when we become one with Christ. But every part of us becomes fully saturated and permeated, as if Christ Jesus is infused into every fiber of our being to make us a light in His kingdom. The indwelling Christ changes our lives forever, and when we step out into the world, it's earthshaking. Apart from the oil of the Spirit, we're like a dry wick and His fire will consume us.[1] Only in the Spirit of Christ are we kindled into a flame to be a light in the world around us.

Twenty-first century Christians are spiritually deprived, even though we hold the complete Scriptures in our hands. Our bookshelves are loaded with several versions of the Bible. Our home libraries hold many Christian self-help books. Teachers and expositors have a plethora of lessons available on YouTube, online, and on TV channels. Inspirational speakers fill stadiums and evangelists hold Bible rallies, but even with all these things readily available, we remain spiritually impoverished. We suffer from a "famine of hearing the words of the Lord."[2]

This spiritual chasm exists because we don't know who we are in Christ. Nor do we understand the fullness of Christ who indwells us. Too often, mature Christians don't know what it means to be in Christ.

It may be obvious to ask: why does Jesus' indwelling presence have to be such a mystery? Mark's Gospel offers a clue. "For whatever is hidden is meant to be disclosed, and whatever is concealed is meant to be brought out into the open."[3] Our heavenly Father reveals Himself to those who search out the mysteries of His kingdom. This study opens our hearts and minds to scriptural evidence to help us sleuth out beautiful truths of this Gospel's mystery.

We are made new creations in Christ by faith. By water and the word, holy baptism unites us with Christ and His body, the Church. Jesus is the gate who opens for us to enter into God's kingdom, and yet too many Christians stop and stand at the threshold—impoverished. We are called to enter into the

---

1. Deuteronomy 4:24.
2. Amos 8:11.
3. Mark 4:22. (Cross reference: Psalm 18:11.)

joy of the fullness of Christ. So, why do we stand with our toes on the threshold of the garden gate and merely observe the bounty of the Garden of God? We keep learning more and more Bible and Church stuff, but we refuse to enter into the benefits of God's kingdom. Does the unknown frighten us like giants in the land?[4] The Scriptures in this study light the way for us to enter into Christ so that we may be partakers of the fullness of Christ.

This topic speaks in particular to Americans who see themselves as rugged individualists. We like to think of ourselves as mavericks on the open range riding out to conquer the wilderness. But when we abide in Christ, we give up our fierce individuality. We don't lose our identity, but we come together as a community to worship, serve, and minister. Those who desire to be fully in Christ must realize all of us together are one body in Christ. We are part of the molecular structure of the body, melted into the body, melded with the body, infused into the body so we can function in unison with all the parts of the body of Christ. We are not the driving gear of the body, but an element among all the working parts that take their direction, leading, and strength from the Head who is Christ.

This study book occasionally uses the name "Yeshua." This sounds like the name people called Jesus when He walked among them in Israel. His name ties us back to Luke 1:31, when the angel Gabriel was sent to Nazareth to reveal to Mary that she would become a mother and have a son. And he said: "You are to give Him the name Ἰησοῦς Iēsoûs." In shortened form, Yeshua, meaning: Yehovah is Salvation. The chapters may include Yeshua HaMashiach, for Jesus the Anointed One. These historic names help to bring us back to the foundations of our Christian faith. This study sometimes notates God's name as Yahweh, meaning "I AM who I AM." This has its roots in the name pronounced to Moses when he asked, "Suppose I go to the Israelites and say to them, 'The God of your fathers has sent me to you,' and they ask me, 'What is his name?' Then what shall I tell them?"[5]

Put on your sleuthing hat and polish your magnifying glass. Let's begin this search for clues to this mystery using words of the Holy Scriptures to lead us into joyful fellowship that makes us one with Christ.

> *Do your best to present yourself to God as one approved, a worker who does not need to be ashamed and who correctly handles the word of truth.*
>
> (2 Timothy 2:15)

---

4. Numbers 13:27–28.
5. Exodus 3:13. Note: Many of today's Christians want to know the historic names of Creator God and His Son, Jesus. Different authors use various names according to their preference. Name choices may include, Yehovah, YaHoWah, YHWH, or YHVH for God the Father. Names for Jesus include Yeshua, YaHusha, or Y'shua for Jesus. To keep us focused on the topics, this study does not advocate for any one version. Instead, familiar names for God and Jesus are used with few exceptions.

Preparations of a Bride

Key Scripture:

- "I pray that out of his glorious riches he may strengthen you with power through his Spirit in your inner being, so that Christ may dwell in your hearts through faith. And I pray that you, being rooted and established in love, may have power, together with all the Lord's holy people, to grasp how wide and long and high and deep is the love of Christ, and to know this love that surpasses knowledge—that you may be filled to the measure of all the fullness of God." (Ephesians 3:16–19)

Weddings are memorable life events. Every moment is filled with anticipation as the bride and groom prepare themselves for their special day. The father escorts his daughter down the aisle, step by step to a whole new season of life. The act of pledging vows before God and witnesses changes their lives and prepares the way for a man and woman to become one, joined together in a covenant of holy matrimony. To make this day complete, they must leave their parents' home. All other special affections must be left behind forever.

In this study, we'll learn that becoming one with Christ is the effect of faith and the reality of His powerful indwelling. Indeed, we are carried over the threshold to become the bride of Christ. This lesson leads us to repentance for the years we tried to walk with one foot on Jesus' narrow pathway and the other foot on the world's broad and slippery road.

Too often modern-day Christians are like people who unfold an umbrella when life gets stormy, but when their lives are sunny, they put away the covering they have in Christ. This lesson's message makes it clear that we cannot walk in the light and in darkness. We cannot remain one in Yeshua, our Lord and Savior, while living a double life. We must count the world's attractions as nothing to keep our eyes focused on the Bridegroom's return.

In the power of the Word and the Holy Spirit we are filled to the full measure of Christ. Then we must remain in Christ, abide in Christ, and be saturated with the oil of the Spirit so that we may shine out as the light of the world. Yes, our feet will slip from Jesus' narrow path, but when we do, our hearts break, we grieve and confess our sin, then receive forgiveness and cleansing so that we may once again fully abide in Christ.

Various metaphors help to open our minds and hearts to this study topic on the realities of being one in Christ and His body, the Church.

> Study Prayer:
>
> *Lord Jesus, show us your ways, and teach us your paths.*
>
> A prayer according to Psalm 25:4

In the beginning, the Word spoke grace, mercy, and forgiveness into being with these beautiful words: "Let there be light." In this powerful proclamation there was love to cover Adam and Eve even after their fall. They suffered great consequences for violating their covenant with their Creator. God banished them from the garden. Adam had to make a living by sweat and hard toil. Eve bore her children in pain. They came under death's curse and all creation became subject to decay. But the first couple received God's mercy and He offered a covering for their transgressions.[1]

Under the New Covenant we have an even greater hope. When we see our depravity, we come to Christ in sin: bent, broken, and with grieving hearts. He advocates for us before the Father and we receive forgiveness for our offenses. But Jesus' New Covenant promise is that our sins are not just covered, but cleansed away. We are separated from our transgressions as far as the East is from the West.[2]

> *If we confess our sins, he is faithful and just and will forgive us our sins and purify us from all unrighteousness.*

(1 John 1:9)

After a son or daughter joins the army, mom will send messages to remind them of important things like, "Always be sure you wear clean white underwear." Her advice is an up close and personal kind of real-life wisdom. (She doesn't have to know that all Army issued garments are olive drab green.) It's a centuries old custom to write to those we love who are far away.

The Apostle John wrote a letter to the church reminding them of important and personal truths. They must resist the temptations of this world. He wrote to fallible people with words of great wisdom and empathy. He knew

---

[1] 1 Peter 4:8.
[2] Psalm 103:12.

they would trip up. He had no doubt that their feet could slip from Jesus' narrow pathway. Because of this, he comforted His followers, reminding them Christ Jesus is their Advocate. He promised to come before the Father on their behalf to declare, "I paid the debt of their sin in full. Let them be forgiven and cleansed." Through Christ's intercessions on our behalf, we are restored to right relationship with the Father. We are clothed with the righteousness of Jesus Christ in clean, white garments.

> *My dear children, I write this to you so that you will not sin. But if anybody does sin, we have an advocate with the Father–Jesus Christ, the Righteous One. He is the atoning sacrifice for our sins, and not only for ours but also for the sins of the whole world.*

(1 John 2:1–2)

The most powerful bonding agents in the kingdom of heaven are faith, hope, and love. It's as if we blend these elements using ¼ cup of faith, ¼ cup of hope, and ½ cup of love. Love is the primary ingredient for keeping us unified with Christ and His body, the Church. Working out our salvation is like adding these good things together. With faith, hope, and love in the mix our bonds are strengthened. These bonding agents keep us in union as one in Christ Jesus.

Love binds us together in a bond of fellowship.[3] Saving faith in God's only Son makes us one family called by God's holy name. How good and pleasant is our great hope in Jesus Christ because it unifies us and brings us into fellowship with the Father, Son, and Holy Spirit.[4] In fact, the Word, who is Jesus Christ, is the glue that holds all creation together.[5] Now, we can work in agreement with Him and be joined together in one body, one faith, and one holy baptism. Be sure to keep these ingredients close at hand to strengthen the bond that holds us in intimate fellowship with Christ Jesus and His body, the Church.

> *And now these three remain: faith, hope and love. But the greatest of these is love.*

(1 Corinthians 13:13)

We're often tempted to make things happen by our own effort alone. We get tired of waiting for heaven to act on our behalf and we shoulder the burden on our own. We tackle the work of ministry like the guy who tucks in his wool plaid shirt, grabs his long handle ax, and works up a sweat splitting firewood. But workers in the kingdom of heaven are to be like the priests who

---

3. Colossians 3:14.
4. Psalm 133:1.
5. Colossians 1:17, Hebrews 1:3.

wear linen to keep them from sweating while they serve. Perspiration is not the means to an eternal victory.[6] As priests who serve in our gatherings for worship, we are called to fully depend on the Spirit of Christ who works in and through us to accomplish Yahweh's good and eternal purpose.

As we worship, serve, and minister before Yeshua, our High Priest, faith, hope, and love make us a cohesive unit in Christ. We're like a team that is unified by these powerful bonding agents, each serving according to their spiritual gift in the power and strength of the Spirit. We submit to others who also serve according to the office or talent given to them. No one tries to exalt themselves above others. If we do try, we'll be like a quarterback who throws the ball and then pushes his tight end out of the way to catch his own pass. That's not a winning strategy.

We must not depend on mortal strengths to do what can only be accomplished by the indwelling Spirit, and in accord with the fruit of the Spirit.

> *For in Christ Jesus neither circumcision nor uncircumcision has any value. The only thing that counts is faith expressing itself through love.*

(Galatians 5:6)

When the reality of Christ confronts us, we are quick to see our need to confess selfish ambitions, self-reliance, and our impatience. A change of heart leads us to admit the harm we've done with our angry words and self-serving acts. We can put spitefulness, fickleness, and unfaithfulness behind us. By the power of the Word and the Holy Spirit our hearts are broken and our eyes are opened to see our need of forgiveness and mercy. The process of bringing our sin to light, calling our hearts to repentance, being forgiven and then cleansed, is like pruning our branches back, so we can be fruitful once again in the kingdom of heaven.

The fruit we used to bear was like the bitter produce of wild olive branches. We were like fig trees that grew nothing but leaves. Weeds choked out the seed of faith that struggled to grow in our lives. But in the Spirit of Christ and in the fullness of Christ, this all changed. We are made like fruitful trees in the garden of God.

> *But the fruit of the Spirit is love, joy, peace, forbearance, kindness, goodness, faithfulness.*

(Galatians 5:22)

If you submerged yourself to the earth's deepest depths, climbed to the highest heights, and rocketed through space to far reaches of the universe, all

---
6. Ezekiel 44:18, Leviticus 16:4.

these vast wonders would offer just a small sample of the greatness of God's love for His people. If you could think faster and know more facts than the best artificial intelligence, your knowledge wouldn't come close to the awesome vastness and power of God's love for His own.

Yahweh, our God, gives us His holy name as He adopts us into His family. The vast riches of heaven are poured out upon the sheep of His pasture to strengthen us as one flock, one Church. Our feet are set upon the Rock, Christ Jesus, where we are anchored together as one in Him. Together we are like one vessel into which He pours a full measure of His loving kindness.

> *For this reason I kneel before the Father, from whom every family in heaven and on earth derives its name. I pray that out of his glorious riches he may strengthen you with power through his Spirit in your inner being, so that Christ may dwell in your hearts through faith. And I pray that you, being rooted and established in love, may have power, together with all the Lord's holy people, to grasp how wide and long and high and deep is the love of Christ, and to know this love that surpasses knowledge–that you may be filled to the measure of all the fullness of God.*

(Ephesians 3:14-19)

This is a beautiful truth. Those who dwell in Christ have a compelling desire to live according to God's precepts. This love-inspired obedience is the product of being bound together in Christ. With this in mind, listen to and watch as a metronome clicks its rhythm. It marks perfect time as if swinging its pendulum from love to obedience—obedience and love. This is a great rhythm for a Christian's walk of faith. We can keep our steps in tune with the Spirit. Love and obey—obey and love.

The Apostle Paul instructs us to examine ourselves to see if we are truly in the faith.[7] The imagery of a metronome offers us one more tool for checking up on our walk of faith. We can ask ourselves, "Am I living in rhythm with the Spirit of Christ who indwells me?"

> *The one who keeps God's commands lives in him, and he in them. And this is how we know that he lives in us: We know it by the Spirit he gave us.*

(1 John 3:24)

Consider a guy who wants to look like he's a Southern California beach boy. You know the type. Canvas shoes with no socks, board shorts, sun-faded shirt, the latest shades, and a surfboard rack on top of his car. But it's all a fantasy because he's stuck with riding a bus to get around in Detroit's projects and doesn't have a way to get to the sunny, sandy beaches in SoCal.

---

7. 2 Corinthians 13:5.

We call ourselves Christians, want to appear as Christian, talk the Christian talk, and sport a John 3:16 t-shirt when we go to church. But after we brush our teeth on Monday morning, we cover it all up with our death metal hoodie and get right back in the rut.[8] But a Christians' life cannot be compartmentalized. If we walk in love, according to God's love, we are called to live in love. This means we ought to live in agreement with the Lord Almighty who is holy and indwells us. To remain in Christ, we must separate ourselves to Christ and live in harmony with all love, righteousness, justice, and peace. We can't live a Sunday life and a very different Monday life and expect to remain in Christ. But even in giant Detroit potholes there is great hope. If we're stuck in a Monday pothole, Christ Jesus is the way out, and it is the way of love, forgiveness, cleansing, and mercy.

> *And so we know and rely on the love God has for us. God is love. Whoever lives in love lives in God, and God in them.*
>
> (1 John 4:16)

Is your life out of rhythm? Does the duplicity of your life create a lot of conflict? Is the hope of your childlike faith shattered? You worked hard to build a better life, but there's no solid foundation to build on and what you built crumbles around you. The winds of tragedy and upheaval rock your boat and you can't stay afloat any longer. You throw out an anchor, but there's no rock to hold you steady.

Then when your heart stops racing for a moment, you hear a knock on your heart's door. You have no strength or desire to answer the door. Then something deep inside compels you to get up and see who is knocking. You open up to the One who has come to shepherd you through the rest of your life. You're not sure why, but you invite Him in to share a meal and listen to His life-giving words—redemptive words, comforting words, life-changing words, and faith-filled words. You know your life will never be the same because He adopts you and gives you His family name. For once you have hope and strength. There is a Rock where you can anchor your life. You can look to Christ the rejected stone who is now the Capstone—a precious cornerstone where you can rebuild your life.[9]

> *Here I am! I stand at the door and knock. If anyone hears my voice and opens the door, I will come in and eat with that person, and they with me.*
>
> (Revelation 3:20)

---

8. Titus 1:16.
9. Isaiah 28:16, Mark 12:10.

The prophet Ezekiel draws a vivid picture of a lost, discarded soul who is redeemed. She is washed and cleansed, and then adorned as a bride. She is prepared with fine jewelry of precious stones, gold and silver. The bride is given the finest linen to wear and the best leather sandals for her feet.[10] Her redemption was prepared in the beginning of creation and is now proclaimed to all who will hear and receive. These awesome words, "Let there be light," serve like a bonding agent to bind us to Christ, as one with Christ. The first words of creation call us to faith, hope, and love that adorn us as a bride for Yeshua, our Bridegroom.

Powerful words spoken in the beginning of time are greater than all the failings of fallible people. They are words of grace, mercy and forgiveness—restorative words, cleansing words, and uplifting words. We can never accomplish what Christ Jesus calls us to do by our own words or efforts. Our own sweat accomplishes nothing of eternal value. Instead, we put on the linen garments of a priest to worship, serve, and minister in the power and strength of the Spirit of Christ.[11]

The Bible offers another word picture: an image of a wild olive branch grafted in to bear good and eternal fruit in the garden of God.[12] The Bridegroom pours into us a full measure of His loving kindness that inspires us to love and obedience. His love compels us to walk as Jesus walked, and it serves like glue to keep us as one with Christ and His body. This isn't just a matter of trying to maintain a Christian veneer, but to live in true harmony with the Light of Life. Even if our lives become shattered, our Lord and Savior is faithful and just to forgive us and cleanse us. He will come to knock on our heart's door. He holds the key in hand as He waits for us to answer His call. The Good Shepherd brings us home, restores our hope, and gives us a Rock where we can anchor our lives. And then He makes us one with Him as He prepares us as a bride living in expectation of the Bridegroom's return.

---

10. Ezekiel 16:4–14.
11. Ezekiel 44:18.
12. Romans 11:17,24.

Chapter 1

Preparations of a Bride

Q & A

1. What is the promise of Christ our Advocate?
   _____
   _____
   _____

2. What are the bonding agents that affect our union with Christ?
   _____
   _____
   _____

3. Describe a Christian's life with Christ who indwells us. Why is it important for us to also abide in Him?
   _____
   _____
   _____

4. Will you answer the knock on your heart's door? Recall the day you answered His knock.
   _____
   _____
   _____

My Journal Notes:

One in Christ

Key Scriptures:

- "Therefore, since we have been justified through faith, we have peace with God through our Lord Jesus Christ, through whom we have gained access by faith into this grace in which we now stand. And we boast in the hope of the glory of God. Not only so, but we also glory in our sufferings, because we know that suffering produces perseverance; perseverance, character; and character, hope. And hope does not put us to shame, because God's love has been poured out into our hearts through the Holy Spirit, who has been given to us." (Romans 5:1–5)

- "Just as sin reigned in death, so also grace might reign through righteousness to bring eternal life through Jesus Christ our Lord." (Romans 5:21)

This chapter is presented as a homily.[1] The key Scriptures guide us through this lesson with instruction that reveals what it means to be "in Christ." Knowing who we are in Christ is an important truth that prepares us for the remaining sessions that take us into an assurance of oneness with Christ. We'll learn the joy and benefits of this union with our Savior, and the bountiful strength that is ours as we live our lives in agreement with our Lord and Savior who indwells us.

> Study Prayer:
>
> *Holy Spirit, guide us in your truth and teach us,*
> *for you are God our Savior, and our hope is in you all day long.*
>
> A prayer according to Psalm 25:5

We are made one with Christ in the waters of baptism and by the Word. By the power of His blood, shed on the cross, we are cleansed so that we may be one with our Savior. We are made righteous in His righteousness so that,

---
1. A homily is a discourse, instruction, or sermon.

in Him, we may show His goodness, declaring the Good News to all who will hear. By the power of Jesus' obedient sacrifice, dying in our place and for our sin, we are brought out of darkness to bask in the light of Christ. By grace and through faith we come to know Jesus the Christ as our Lord and Savior. As we hear the word, we are given ears to grasp the truth of the Gospel. Truth convicts our hearts, and by faith we are fused together as one with our Savior. Then Yahweh, our Lord and God, becomes a living reality in every moment of our lives.

When we come into covenant with Christ, our Bridegroom, we are joined as one with the Father, Son, and Holy Spirit. This is true fidelity with our Lord and Savior. In Yeshua, our Redeemer, we are brought into a peaceful tranquility that shields us from the world's chaos and brings us into a peaceful kingdom—the garden of God's rest. Our Savior's every attribute and all that He is indwells us. David sang out with a Psalm declaring the joy of those who are joined as one with the Lord.

They feast on the abundance of your house; you give them drink from your river of delights.

(Psalm 36:8)

By means of the cross of Jesus Christ, we gain a sense of belonging. We have been bought with a price, and now our lives have a Rock in whom we are anchored. Indeed, He holds us in His loving arms. In Him we have a tried-and-true foundation to build our lives on. We become a people who have a lasting and eternal hope. By faith, through the waters of baptism, we are joined with Christ in His suffering, death, and the power of resurrection. We were once cast off, but now our Savior holds us close—so close that we are one with Him, inseparable from His body, the Church.

In Christ we have access into Yahweh's holy presence. We come boldly before the throne of grace because we are encompassed in our Lord and Savior. When truth convicts us and we live accordingly, our relationship with our Creator is restored. By grace through faith, we now abide in Christ to make a powerful union. He fills us with the joy of heaven's delights and the pleasures of fellowship and community. We come to know the full measure of His loving kindness. We are given favor in the kingdom of heaven. Freedom in the bountiful paradise of God is ours because we are one with our Lord and Savior.

In Christ we are strengthened to stand firm upon the Rock. He gives us a foundation stone to build our lives on. We are given a new family name, the name of the Lord Almighty. Then we come to know the power and authority of His name that is given to us. When Christ indwells us, and we abide in Him, we are compelled to exalt and glorify God on account of the mighty work He has accomplished in us. We can live a life of great expectation, ready to enter into the eternal home He is preparing for us. Godly confidence is obvious in every step we take as we remain true to the Author of our hope who lives in us. Jesus' own words assure us.

> *And if I go and prepare a place for you, I will come back and take you to be with me that you also may be where I am.*
>
> (John 14:3)

We hold fast in Christ and submit to Him as Lord and King so we may see more and more of His majesty, splendor, and the brightness of His glorious light. We glory in Christ in every circumstance. Whether our farms or gardens flourish with abundance or wither from drought, we continue to lift up holy hands to exalt God who provides.[2]

Entering into the fullness of Christ means that we are brought into His suffering and death. As part of the body of Christ, we are called to finish the work of His suffering through afflictions and tribulations wreaked upon His Church.[3] We are called to take up the cross of Jesus Christ for the cause of the Gospel. Those who are in Christ can rejoice in suffering because we know the victorious end result of the church's persecutions. Paul taught this truth in his epistle to the Romans.

> *Now if we are children, then we are heirs–heirs of God and co-heirs with Christ, if indeed we share in his sufferings in order that we may also share in his glory.*
>
> (Romans 8:17)

In Christ and His suffering, a great work is accomplished in us: we overcome the world and the darkness is driven back.[4] In suffering we become steadfast in the Word and patient in tribulation. We are strengthened to endure as we wait for the Bridegroom to return for His own. He is our strength so that we will not falter. In His strength we remain faithful to His church even while enduring trials that afflict us. We stand strong in the faith to proclaim the Good News of the kingdom of heaven. In the darkest moments when evil assaults us, we can rise up with confident expectation of our Salvation. Our character is tested in tribulations, tried, and proven strong so we may hold fast to the Author of our hope. For those who abide in Christ, this great expectation keeps us from sinking into dishonor and shame. Ungod-

---

2. Habakkuk 3:17–18.
3. Colossians 1:24.
4. 1 John 2:8.

ly people will attempt to discredit and humiliate us, but their vicious words are nothing more than smoke that soon blows away with the wind.[5]

Enduring strength is made possible because God's overwhelming love is poured out to flood our heart and soul. This is the work of the Holy Spirit who is the wind breathed into us—the breath of life. We are given the Spirit of Grace who bestows abundant measures of affection, good will, and favor upon us. These good things are ours because of God's faithfulness. In Christ we can persevere, holding fast to this great hope. Our character is refined in fiery trials that fortify us. All the essence of the Spirit of Christ is generously poured into us as if filling jars of clay with the oil of love, strength, peace, and comfort. All those who are anointed and called by His holy name are precious vessels fit to serve their purpose in the kingdom of heaven. Indeed, we are cleansed to serve.

> *How much more, then, will the blood of Christ, who through the eternal Spirit offered himself unblemished to God, cleanse our consciences from acts that lead to death, so that we may serve the living God!*

(Hebrews 9:14)

Jesus gave His followers a Great Commission which, on our own, is an impossible mission. We are called to work in His harvest field and "bring in the sheaves."[6] This good work is to bring lost souls into the kingdom of heaven so they may rest in pleasant pastures and delight in the sweetness and favor the Lord Almighty. His sheep were once lost but now found and brought home to the blessings of His merciful kindness and made one with us in Christ.

This is a bountiful kingdom where our God reigns supreme. He is our Lord, and Master of our lives. By the power of His word, we walk in the light of Christ. Our lives are no longer controlled by our sinful nature, but ruled by the Spirit of God who indwells us.[7] As the Spirit of Jesus reigns in us, we are set apart, made acceptable so that we may come boldly before the Father and lay our petitions before Him. Our Lord Jesus, who is without beginning or end, brings us into the fullness of life. He makes new creations of all who come to Him by faith, and who believe that His body was broken so that we might be healed in body, soul, and spirit. We come with confident assurance that His blood was shed for forgiveness and cleansing of our sin. We press in, assured by the Scriptures that He is the first fruits of resurrection. Death is

---

5. Psalm 68:2.
6. Psalm 126:6.
7. Romans 8:9

defeated and we will be raised up in Christ.[8] This cleansing is life-changing because it washes us to the very depths of our soul. Yeshua HaMachiash is the anointed One who is Sovereign over every aspect of our lives. Our Lord and Savior brings His people together as one in a bond of fellowship, transcending all boundaries to make us one with Him. His vicarious sacrifice brings us to live together united in Christ. The Psalmist looked forward to this joyful truth.

> *How good and pleasant it is when God's people live together in unity!*

(Psalm 133:1)

A clear word of counsel serves to keep us on the right track. Our covenant bond is a two-way relationship. As an example: a marriage with one spouse married and the other living like they're single never works. We are pledged to Yeshua, our Bridegroom, and we ought to live as His bride, keeping ourselves pure. We are a people set apart as a holy nation and a royal priesthood.[9]

Consider the precious words Ruth spoke to Naomi, pledging fidelity with her as one family. She made this vow as they set out to take Naomi back to her homeland.

> *Where you go, I will go, and where you stay I will stay. Your people will be my people and your God my God. Where you die, I will die, and there I will be buried. May the Lord deal with me, be it ever so severely, if even death separates you and me.*

(Ruth 1:16–17)

Ruth's promise reminds us of the powerful pledge of faithfulness we make as followers of Christ. An oath of faithfulness binds us together as one. Her devotion teaches us that when we offer our lives to Christ as His disciple it is a "where you die, I will die" and a "where you live, I will live" kind of relationship.

An earnest vow doesn't make us one with Christ, but it is the reality of all those who are united in Him. Our Lord Jesus, by the sacrifice of His body and the shedding of His blood, made a way for us to become one with Him. Look at the powerful effect of Jesus' body, broken so that we might be made whole. One great reality of this truth is that we are united in a covenant community—the body of Christ.

---

8. 1 Corinthians 15:20.
9. 1 Peter 2:9.

Consider how Jesus made this unity possible. A soldier ripped His back with a cat-of-nine-tails. They drove nails through His hands and feet, and pierced His side with a Roman spear. They tore His body so severely that He was barely recognizable as human.[10] He submitted to the horrors so that His body, the Church, might be made whole—many parts but one unbroken body—embodied in Him. One Head. One Church.

Is it right to say that in order to be one with Christ we must take part in a local church? The Scriptures compel us to assemble to worship, serve, and minister before the Lord. But submissive and obedient acts of joining in with corporate worship, by themselves, do not make us one with Christ. Instead, they are the evidence, the fruit of those who are in Christ. He made us one in Him by grace through faith. We enter into Yeshua, our Savior, by believing in His saving grace and vicarious suffering, death, and resurrection.

In truth, being in Christ is to flourish, blossom out, and bear the fruit of faith. When we come to saving faith, we enter into a powerful and dynamic covenant with Christ who dwells in us. Christ's inner activating power compels us to worship, serve, and live in harmony with His holy presence. Living in agreement with Christ who indwells us is the essence of abiding in Christ. This unity is the core of our covenantal relationship. The Psalmist expresses this truth beautifully.

> *Happy are those who hear the joyful call to worship, for they will walk in the light of your presence, Lord.*

(Psalm 89:15 NLT)

The faith of our forefather Abraham offers an example to teach us what it means to be in Christ who indwells us. When we pray for the Lord to touch and heal us, it makes sense to act in agreement with what we pray. We pray for our strained back in agreement with God's promises, and stop lifting hundred-pound boxes until our back is strong again. We pray and then act in accord with Christ Jesus who is the "Yes" and the "Amen."

Abraham's life shows us the powerful effect of this awesome oneness. The Lord of all heaven and earth brought Abram into covenant with Him and gave him a new name, Abraham.[11] Abraham put feet to his faith to search for a city with foundations established in the beginning of creation and whose architect and builder is God.[12] But he saw only a shadow of what was to come—that is the coming Messiah.[13] Today, the God of Abraham gathers His

---

10. Isaiah 52:14.
11. Abram means exalted father, and Abraham means father of many nations.
12. Hebrews 11:10.
13. Colossians 2:17.

people as a holy nation in covenant with the Great I AM. Under this new and better covenant, "we have come to Mount Zion, the heavenly Jerusalem, the city of the living God." The veil in the temple was torn in two so that all those who are one in Christ may enter the Most Holy Place.[14] We stand before the Father with great confidence because we come in the person of our Savior who mediates on our behalf as High Priest. When the Almighty looks upon us, He sees Christ in us, and us in Christ.

We are God's people, set apart and made a holy nation of priests. The Church is separated to Christ so we may spread the Good News and serve God's holy and eternal purpose. We are joined together as one body with our Lord Jesus who indwells us as we abide in Him. By the power of the Word and the anointing of the Holy Spirit we minister, serve, and worship, joined together as one with the Almighty. We are one with Him in His trials and tribulations so that we may complete the work of the Church. In the waters of holy baptism and by the power of the Word we are made new creations in Christ, buried with our Savior, and raised up with Him in resurrection power. We are given a new name, a family name that joins us with Him. Now, in the work of the Church and the Great Commission, we are his voice to speak out what He is speaking. We are His hands extended to all whom He touches. Indeed, we are one with Christ, and we are called to live in agreement with His holy indwelling presence. Our submissive lifestyle affects everything our hands touch, what we feast our eyes on, and the thoughts we entertain.[15] We are to live as His light in the world and be the salt that preserves. We are the bride who is pledged to the Bridegroom who has gone to prepare an eternal home for all those who abide in Christ.

---

14. Hebrews 10:19–20.
15. This truth was foreshadowed in Yehovah's command to observe the Passover feast in Exodus 13:9.

Chapter 2
One in Christ
Q & A

1. How are we made new creations who are one with Christ?
   _____
   _____
   _____

2. How does Christ's indwelling presence give us the boldness to approach the Throne of Grace?
   _____
   _____
   _____

3. What is the impact on our lives as Christians when we abide in Christ?
   _____
   _____
   _____

4. What does Ruth's pledge to Naomi teach us about our union with Christ?
   _____
   _____
   _____

My Journal Notes:

Confidence and Assurance

Key Scriptures:

- "For no matter how many promises God has made, they are 'Yes' in Christ. And so through him the 'Amen' is spoken by us to the glory of God." (2 Corinthians 1:20)

- "We want each of you to show this same diligence to the very end, so that what you hope for may be fully realized." (Hebrews 6:11)

All of God's promises are "Yes" for those who abide in Christ. Our heavenly Father does not answer His promises with, "Yes, no, or maybe later." Indeed, our Lord Jesus is the "Amen" to every one of God's promises.[1] We approach the Throne of Grace with great confidence, knowing that through an abundance of grace and mercy we are ushered in by our High Priest, Jesus the Son of God.[2] In Christ we stand before a holy God covered with a sure Promise that is confirmed with an oath.[3]

This chapter serves to build our confident assurance and prepare us to come boldly before the Father of Light. We know that we are recipients of all that He has promised to those who remain in Christ. The joy of our salvation is restored to us as we come with contrite hearts, covered in the blessings of our Habitation, who is Jesus the Christ.

Study Prayer:

*Abba Father, teach us your ways,
lead us in a straight path because of our oppressors.*

A prayer according to Psalm 27:11

---

1. Revelation 3:14.
2. Hebrews 4:14–16.
3. Hebrews 6:17.

The certainty of our eternal hope rests in Christ who is the anchor for our soul.[4] We have a sure promise of redemption and we enter into this promise by means of Christ's suffering and death on a cruel Roman cross. Yeshua is the Lamb of God who brings us into the Father's rest by means of resurrection power. In the waters of baptism, by the power of the Word, we are brought into Christ: his suffering, death, and resurrection. The power of water separated for this holy purpose, together with the sure promises of the Word, make us one in Christ. We are brought into covenant with Christ and assured of His great and eternal promises. Our part of the covenant is to remain in Him, abide in Him, and keep our feet on the path He sets before us. This constancy is only possible in the strength and power of the Spirit, the light of the holy Scriptures, love-compelled obedience, and a contrite heart.

> *The works of his hands are faithful and just; all his precepts are trustworthy. They are established for ever and ever, enacted in faithfulness and uprightness. He provided redemption for his people; he ordained his covenant forever–holy and awesome is his name.*

(Psalm 111:7–9)

All people who come to saving faith come by no effort of their own. They are true children of an Abraham-and-Sarah kind of faith. Saying the perfect prayer of confession with the right words doesn't save us if not combined with faith. Water that is set apart for a holy purpose does not save us if not combined with faith in Jesus Christ. We are called to believe that Jesus is the Son of God who died and shed His blood to take away the sins of the world.

Our salvation is by grace through faith and not by means of anything we do. But keep in mind that this faith is powerfully redemptive and spurs us to act.[5] Abraham, by faith, gathered his family, packed up his tent, and made the trek to a land he knew nothing about. Then, by faith, he waited upon the Lord for twenty-five years before Sarah gave birth to the promised son, Isaac. In essence, his faith compelled him to wait and act in agreement.

> *Therefore, the promise comes by faith, so that it may be by grace and may be guaranteed to all Abraham's offspring–not only to those who are of the law but also to those who have the faith of Abraham. He is the father of us all.*

(Romans 4:16)

How can we know and be confident in the truth? This assurance comes from the power of the Word and the indwelling Holy Spirit who opens the Scriptures to us. It's clear and simple. The Holy Spirit inspired words for the

---
4. Hebrews 6:19.
5. James 2:22.

apostles and prophets to record, and now this same Spirit opens our understanding to His inspired words in the Bible. The great mystery of all Gospel truth is opened to all who will listen to the voice of the Spirit who instructs us.

By the power of the Spirit of Grace, we are led to walk in the light of truth. Growing in grace and knowledge is a matter of taking steps of faith. We begin learning by taking small steps first so we can move on to take bigger steps.

Step 1: Listen, search the Scriptures to learn what is true and right.

Step 2: Repent and then walk according to the truth we know.

Step 3: Repeat, again and again and again until the day the good Lord calls us home.

But you have an anointing from the Holy One, and all of you know the truth. (1 John 2:20)

The Bible uses many word pictures to help us see ourselves as a people who dwell in the shelter of the Almighty. We are also likened to a house that He inhabits. All God's people together are like a tent where He takes up residence. Those who are called by His name are a cleansed and sanctified temple where the Holy Spirit dwells with holy fire. The sons and daughters of the Most High God are called to serve as vessels for the fire of the Spirit. Christ Jesus has bought us at a price for this very purpose. We are called to saving faith in Jesus Christ and made into vessels for the oil of the Holy Spirit. This is a great mystery we are searching out. It is the hope of our glory.[6]

The inspired Scriptures also show us that all whose names are written in the Book of Life are called to abide in the Father's tent where we take refuge. We find shelter under His wings.[7] He is our sanctuary. Our safe haven. Our Lord God shields us and hides us in the shelter of His sacred tent. The Lord of Glory is our fortress, a shelter where we may dwell in safety and rest in the Shadow of the Almighty. This hope anchors us to remain in Christ. This promise brings us intimately near and sanctified to dwell in the Father's courts on His holy mountain.[8] Now, in Christ, we enter the Most Holy Sanctuary where the curtain was torn to give us access. This is the place where we abide in Yahweh's holy presence. This is the place where we dwell in safety and stand in God's council so that we may know Him, His heart, His counsels, and His thoughts.[9]

---

6. In order of reference: Hebrews 3:6, Psalm 91:10, John 14:17, 1 John 4:15, 1 Corinthians 6:19-20, Isaiah 32:18, Colossians 1:27.
7. See Chapter 11, "Love's Promise," in the author's book: The Greatest Love.
8. Hebrews 12:22–24.
9. In order of reference: John 15:4, Psalm 91:4, Psalm 43:2, Psalm 46:11, Psalm 91:1, Psalm 65:4, Hebrews 6:18-20, Hebrews 8:1-2.

Your statutes, Lord, stand firm; holiness adorns your house for endless days.

(Psalm 93:5)

Are you searching for an eternally safe place to call home? You find this dwelling place when you hear and believe the power of the promise—God's Word. Now kindle your hunger and thirst for the holy Scriptures and they will light your path. Dig into every word written in the Bible because they are spirit and life.[10] Be a diligent student in search of the mysteries of the Gospel because these are the words of eternal life.[11]

The Word is Jesus Christ, the Rock on whom every safe and unshakable dwelling place is built. Your life may be pummeled by pandemics, earthquakes, wildfires, political upheaval, or loss of good health, but you have a sure and lasting promise that can never be taken away.[12]

Heaven and earth will pass away, but my words will never pass away.

(Luke 21:33)

Resting in the Lord is not a matter of turning off your cell phone, going to church on Sunday morning, having a leisurely lunch with church friends, and then taking a nap before the football game starts. All of these things are fine, but this is not the essence of resting in the Lord.

On the seventh day of creation, the Creator ceased from His work and rested. It's as if He sat down and then patted the seat beside him, saying to all His sons and daughters who would live on created earth: "Come into my rest." His rest relieves us of the burden of having to accomplish the work of the Great Commission on our own; by means of our own strength. Rest means that we no longer trust in the strength of our stellar resume. Being seated with the Father means we count as nothing our gold medals, trophies, and Certificates of Achievement. Entering into rest with our Creator means that we live in the faith of Abraham. Without weakening in our faith, we accept that our bodies are as good as dead, and then by faith live in agreement with the Great I AM who indwells us. By faith even those who are barren burst into song because of their many children.[13] By His strength not one word of hope disappoints and we can be sure that all His promises will come to fruition.[14]

---

10. John 6:63.
11. John 6:68.
12. Habakkuk 3:17–19.
13. Isaiah 54:1.
14. Romans 4:19–24, 5:3–5.

Praise be to the Lord, who has given rest to his people Israel just as he promised. Not one word has failed of all the good promises he gave through his servant Moses.

(1 Kings 8:56)

If a kid wants to go to summer camp, they have to get on the bus. They must board that big yellow people-mover so they can join the clamor and get dropped off at Camp Mosquito by the lake where they'll swim, canoe, play capture the flag, enjoy camp food, and develop some life-long friendships.

The bride of Christ waits for the Bridegroom's return with instructions on how to "get on the bus." The bride-in-waiting is confident and assured of the Bridegroom's love. Every waiting moment is filled with anticipation of the call: "Here's the bridegroom! Come out to meet him!" The bride's waiting isn't just idle moments. She lives a life of preparation, continually being filled and refilled with the oil of the Spirit. She makes ready even as she watches for Him, feeding on the holy words of the Apostles and Prophets and living in agreement with these words every day of her life. She flourishes in the glow of the Bridegroom's love and lives each day by determining her steps according to the light of the word, and then repenting of her missteps. The bride is ready!

Maranatha, come Yeshua HaMashiach.[15]

He who testifies to these things says, "Yes, I am coming soon." Amen. Come, Lord Jesus."

(Revelation 22:20)

Every promise in the Book is "Yes" and "Amen" for all those who live in agreement with Christ. We are established in His promises because of Jesus' submissive obedience, even to His suffering and death on the cross. All the promises are ours by faith—an Abraham kind of faith that doesn't depend on what we do, but spurs us to act according to it.

By means of our Spirit's instruction we come to know the way of truth and righteousness. We open our Bibles to hear precious, strengthening, and healing words. The Spirit of Christ opens our understanding to receive the promises of eternal life and our hearts become confident that these truths will never pass away. When the Word speaks, His voice isn't like ours that fades over a distance. His spoken words are sure, echoing to be heard again and again to the far reaches of the earth throughout all time.

---

15. Maranatha is an Aramaic phrase meaning, "Come, our Lord." Yeshua HaMashiach is Hebrew meaning, "Jesus the Anointed One."

We are confident in God's promises because we rest in the Lord. This is not a Sunday nap kind of rest, but entering into the fullness of Christ and His sure promises. Indeed, we can rest assured that our soon-coming King will return for His bride. Every word of His promises offers us hope, because Yahweh, our heavenly Father, has poured out His love "into our hearts through His Holy Spirit who has been given to us."[16]

How do we "get on the bus?" How can we be assured and secure as we join the joyful ruckus on the bus and wait for the Bridegroom's coming? By the power of the Word and the Holy Spirit we are called to live a life of preparation, getting ourselves ready as a bride, putting on adornments that are treasures of the kingdom of heaven, the precious oil of the Spirit—spiritual gifts freely given as the Spirit determines.

Maranatha, come Lord Jesus.

---

16. Romans 5:4–5.

Chapter 3

Assurance and Confidence

Q & A

1. What steps can you take to know what is right and true?
   _____
   _____
   _____

2. How is it possible to enter into the Father's courtyards on His holy mountain?
   _____
   _____
   _____

3. What is the impact on your life when you enter the Creator's rest?
   _____
   _____
   _____

4. Who is the Rock upon whom you can build a life of faith that is safe and unshakeable?
   _____
   _____
   _____

My Journal Notes:

A Foundation from the Beginning

Key Scripture:

- "As for you, see that what you have heard from the beginning remains in you. If it does, you also will remain in the Son and in the Father. And this is what he promised us—eternal life." (1 John 2:24–25)

Every runner must start a marathon at the beginning. In life's endurance race, whether we come to saving faith on our dying day or live with Christ's covering from the day we're conceived, we start this life of faith at the beginning.[1] The first words of creation, "Let there be light," energize every part of our being as we press on toward the goal to win the prize.[2] These awesome words remain in us to carry us into the presence of the Lord after we gasp for life's last breath.[3] The first words of creation established this foundation and must permeate every fiber of our being. The words of the hymn sung out by the church for centuries remain true: "Glory to the Father, and to the Son, and to the Holy Spirit: as it was in the beginning, is now, and will be forever. Amen."[4]

To open this great mystery, this study takes us to the beginning so we can see the foundation we must build upon. The first words of creation are the bedrock for all good things set in place for all time. The Son's powerful words light the way to the final words of the Messiah who is the Capstone for all God's promises. We'll examine foundational building stones according to truth, righteousness, love, and justice. We'll measure every word by the standard of the Scriptures to confirm that it is complete, right, and true.

---

1. 2 Timothy 2:5.
2. Philippians 3:14.
3. 2 Corinthians 5:8.
4. From the Liturgy of the Hours.

> Study Prayer:
>
> *Teach us your way, O Lord, that we may rely on your faithfulness. Give us undivided hearts, that we may fear your name.*
>
> A prayer according to Psalm 86:11

The first words of creation are vital, pointing the way for the revelation of Jesus Christ. The Alpha spoke, "Let there be light." In the final word of Scripture, the Omega proclaims His great promise, "Yes, I am coming soon." The Apostle John's words proclaim his agreement, "Amen. Come, Lord Jesus."[5] Now look up, for Christ victorious comes as flashing lightning, visible from east to west.[6]

Let's examine what existed as the Word spoke creation's first miraculously powerful words. The Alpha, who is the beginning and end, commanded and all things became established.[7] Before time began there was grace. The Holy Spirit breathed into the nostrils of the man who was formed from the dust of the ground and he became a living being.[8] The Spirit of Grace existed before the beginning of time as life-giving wind—the breath of life.

The breath of life filled the man Adam with grace. And now the Spirit's grace calls us to live a life that is set apart to Christ Jesus our Lord and Savior. The man formed from the dust laid lifeless on the ground and the Spirit breathed life into him. In the same way, we were dead in our sins[9] and the Spirit of Grace breathed life into us—His undeserved gift to lift us up and give us life forevermore.

> *He has saved us and called us to a holy life–not because of anything we have done but because of his own purpose and grace. This grace was given us in Christ Jesus before the beginning of time.*

(2 Timothy 1:9)

Yeshua, our Savior, is the personification of all wisdom. He is the Word that spoke and all things were created. The Son of God was there to speak words of wisdom before the mountains and hills were set in place. Christ Jesus was and is the embodiment of all wisdom. The Word of wisdom was there when Creator God drew a circle on the face of the deep that came to order as

---

5. Revelation 22:20.
6. Matthew 24:27.
7. Psalm 33:9.
8. Genesis 2:7.
9. Ephesians 2:1.

created earth.[10] With Wisdom at His side, the Master Builder set the foundations of the earth in place for all time.

Creator God established wisdom as He set everything in place for the created earth and its inhabitants. By His Word He established all that is wise and good for all time. In wisdom, the Creator set in place the distinctions between right and wrong, light and darkness. This is a solid and eternal foundation for us to build our lives on.

> *We declare God's wisdom, a mystery that has been hidden and that God destined for our glory before time began.*
>
> (1 Corinthians 2:7)

Before Wisdom spoke light into being, our names were written in the Book of Life. We have an awesome joy, a confident assurance, knowing our name is recorded in indelible ink. The Father wrote our names down in glory even before our ancestors Adam and Eve were created. With our names written in the Book of Life we have a covering, a shield that keeps us sheltered under Jesus' wings[11] until the end of time. We will not waver. We must not falter. Those who are one in Christ can stand firm on His promises and only observe with our eyes while the names of the enemies of Christ our Messiah are blotted out.[12]

We have no fear of falling prey to end-time wrath because we are covered by the blood of the Lamb of God who was slain. His blood sacrifice was effective from the very foundations of the earth. His vicarious sacrifice provided a covering for Adam and Eve after they broke their covenant with the Father. Because of His abounding love, the Creator provided animal skins to serve as a covering for their sin. Is it possible that Creator God slayed a lamb to provide their coverings?[13] This act of grace would be consistent with the types and images of Messiah in the Old Testament.

Jesus' sacrificial death and resurrection are timeless, reaching back through time to the beginning, redeeming us in our day and time, and stretching forward to the very end.

> *All inhabitants of the earth will worship the beast—all whose names have not been written in the Lamb's book of life, the Lamb who was slain from the creation of the world.*
>
> (Revelation 13:8)

---

10. Proverbs 8:27.
11. The tassels on the corner of a Jewish prayer shawl are referred to as "Wings." Jesus' intercessions on our behalf cover us like wings. See John 17.
12. Psalm 91:8.
13. Genesis 3:21.

Before time began the promise of eternal life was fixed in place. This is a well-established and unbreakable promise that reaches back to earth's foundation and extends forward to the end. We can rest assured that this hope cannot be stolen away because it has an eternal foundation. As one in Christ, we have a Rock in whom we anchor that holds us secure while the storms of life and fierce winds of persecution pummel us. The Psalmist offers encouragement for those who cry out to the Lord in their time of need: "From the ends of the earth I call to you, I call as my heart grows faint; lead me to the rock that is higher than I."[14]

The foundations of the earth were set in place with a promise that leads us to a glorious city whose architect and builder is God. By faith we look forward, as if straining our eyes to see this glorious place promised to all those who are one in Christ.

> *Paul, a servant of God and an apostle of Jesus Christ to further the faith of God's elect and their knowledge of the truth that leads to godliness–in the hope of eternal life, which God, who does not lie, promised before the beginning of time.*

(Titus 1:1–2)

This generation continues to chip away at the godly foundations established for this nation. Too many Boomers handed down a legacy of spiritual bankruptcy. These folks created many forms of godliness that made church meaningless because the power of living godly lives is forgotten.[15] The name of Jesus is often proclaimed in our congregations, but the power of His holy name is denied. The Holy Spirit is referenced in sermons, but our leaders deny true gifts of the Spirit for the people. A heap of ashes lies in our wake, leaving our children with a church that is little more than crosses hanging on the wall and stained-glass windows; their true value forgotten. We have left our children with pointless forms of religion.

But our Lord and Savior rises up triumphant to redeem us from our empty spiritual practices. By the power of the blood of the Lamb we are lifted out of the darkness of hollow religion into the light of true and real worship. Yeshua is the tried and precious cornerstone set in place at the foundation of creation and remains as the Rock to build upon so that we may enter into worship that is spiritual and real.

---

14. Psalm 61:2.
15. 2 Timothy 3:5.

For you know that it was not with perishable things such as silver or gold that you were redeemed from the empty way of life handed down to you from your ancestors, but with the precious blood of Christ, a lamb without blemish or defect. He was chosen before the creation of the world, but was revealed in these last times for your sake.

(1 Peter 1:18–20)

Christ's love is at work in us, compelling us to obey.[16] Before time began, we were set apart as a holy nation, a Church that is conformed to Christ victorious. In the beginning the Creator selected the sheep of His pasture by name, those who would be conformed to Christ. Before the first light blazed out over earth's chaotic mass, we were called to be submitted servants to Christ in His body, the Church. Our submitted obedience is the fruit of the vineyard Jesus spoke of in His parable of the tenants. In Jesus' allegory, the Father sent His one and only Son to collect some of the fruit of the vineyard, but they killed Him and threw Him out.[17] We must ask ourselves, will we crucify Christ again in our day?[18]

It's no accident of choice that we are sons and daughters of the Most High God. No twist of fate made us priests who serve before Yeshua HaMachiash, our High Priest. In Christ, the Church is built with living stones and every part of the body is called to minister as ordained servant priests in the kingdom of heaven. Before time was set for the universe, the Almighty knew us by name and set us apart to serve as sons and daughters of righteousness.

For he chose us in him before the creation of the world to be holy and blameless in his sight.

(Ephesians 1:4)

There is a kingdom beyond anything we could ask or imagine. The treasures of the kingdom of heaven are so abundant that the greatest nations and monarchies on earth that have ever existed cannot compare to the glory of God's eternal sovereignty. We serve a King who rules in splendor, and He prepared an eternal home for us as our inheritance.

With His shepherd's rod, the Son of God judges with justice to separate sheep from the goats. He separates the violent from the peacemakers; those steeped in darkness from those who walk in the light.[19] God's holy people are placed at His right hand to hear His precious words—a blessing prepared for God's holy nation even before the creation of the wildlife, mountains, lakes, rivers, and oceans on this blue-green planet.

---

16. 2 John 1:6.
17. Mark 12:1–11.
18. Hebrews 6:4–6.
19. Ezekiel 34:17.

> *Then the King will say to those on his right, "Come, you who are blessed by my Father; take your inheritance, the kingdom prepared for you since the creation of the world."*

(Matthew 25:34)

Why is it so important to understand what existed before the beginning? Because it is vital for us to know our eternal and omnipresent Redeemer in whom we dwell and who powerfully dwells in us. This is the eternal nature of our heavenly Father who beckons us to enter into the fullness of His being. Our Lord and Savior established a foundation before the beginning of time and this is the bedrock our lives are built upon. What He spoke into being in the beginning established the foundation for everything that comes after.

When societies, halls of justice, governance, home, family, and worship are established upon foundations that existed from day-one of creation, there is order, respect for authority, justice for all, peace in the home, and a people who live peacefully in community.[20]

We test all that is taught by the truth established when the Word of creation spoke; "Let there be light." Now we're ready to build our lives upon the eternal Rock, Christ Jesus. In Christ we have healing, health, abundance, freedom, purpose, and great fruitfulness in the work of the kingdom. Our blessings are greater than we could ever ask or imagine. We are engulfed with all His blessings when we abide in Christ and overcome by the blood of the Lamb of God who takes away the sins of the world. The foundation for all creation is timeless; brought to order, and set in place before time began.

---

20. 1 Timothy 2:1–2.

Chapter 4

A Foundation from the Beginning

Q & A

1. What existed before time began on day one of creation?

_____
_____
_____

2. How does hollow religion impact our nation, culture, and our everyday lives?

_____
_____
_____

3. Why is it important for us to know what existed before the beginning of time?

_____
_____
_____

My Journal Notes:

Created for Fellowship

Key Scriptures:

- "We proclaim to you what we have seen and heard, so that you also may have fellowship with us. And our fellowship is with the Father and with his Son, Jesus Christ." (1 John 1:3)

- "For we are the temple of the living God. As God has said: 'I will live with them and walk among them, and I will be their God, and they will be my people.'" (2 Corinthians 6:16)

In this study we'll clear up misunderstandings about who we are in Christ and our relationship with the Father, Son, and Holy Spirit. We'll begin with the false claim that "God doesn't need us."

Solomon's wisdom teaches us about love and the need it creates through his poetic song. We'll look at the above false statement in light of the Song of Songs. The words of his poetic songs lead us to enjoy the aromas and sweetness of the fruits of love. When we read this with our heart and soul at rest in the Lord, it soon becomes clear that religious speakers who claim, "God doesn't need us," base this teaching on human reasoning. Yes, the Almighty can accomplish all He desires without us—He is more than able. But Solomon makes it clear that Yahweh is a God of covenants and chooses to bring us into His plans.[1] Indeed, where there is love, a need for loved ones blossoms out with a beautiful fragrance.

Study Prayer:

O Lord Almighty, praise be to you, O Lord; teach us your decrees.

A prayer according to Psalm 119:12

We experience a similar love/need relationship when we come to love our spouse. We learn to love them and, before long, we realize that we need them

---
1. Genesis 18:17, Psalm 25:14.

in our lives. Loving our children means that we need them—our lives are incomplete without them. When we send the kids to Grandma and Grandpa's house in the country for two weeks, our hearts burst with a felt need for those noisy little rascals.

A true love is the impulse for the need we have for our beloved. Our Father's love is greater than any love known between created beings here on earth. Because of His love for us, our Creator needs all those who are called by His holy name.

Consider Christ's love for His own. He is the Head of the Church which is His body. Does a Head need a body? That may seem like a ridiculous question, but erroneous thinking has invaded Christendom, eroded our faith and our view of who we are in Christ. Our heavenly Father needs us because He loves us. We respond to this heavenly love by gathering to worship as one people before Christ our High Priest. In our worship assemblies we receive the ministries of Yeshua and then return this love by exalting the Lord, lifting up holy hands in worship, and shouting out with praise for the God of our salvation.[2]

> *I belong to my beloved, and his desire is for me.*

(Song of Songs 7:10)

The Greek word for "will" in the coming verse is: θέλημα thélēma, pronounced thel'-ay-mah. In addition to meaning "what one wishes or determines shall be accomplished," it has clear connotations of yearning and enjoyment. The KJV correctly translated "will" as "for thy pleasure they are and were created." The Creator brought us close to His heart for the purpose of intimate fellowship. This kind of communion is so much more fulfilling than an obligatory one-hour-a-week kind of fellowship. It's a yearning that can't be fulfilled by only celebrating religious holidays. It's a fellowship that permeates every moment of our lives.

Come near to the heart of God. Rest in the Lord and in the power of His might. Enter into the joy of the Lord and His sweet, loving fellowship. We were created for this good purpose—to walk with God in a garden of delights and enjoy the variety of colors, flavors, beauty, and fragrances of love—all that He has created.

> *You are worthy, our Lord and God, to receive glory and honor and power, for you created all things, and by your will they were created and have their being.*

(Revelation 4:11)

---

2. Psalm 71:23.

Some evangelists claim that, "Salvation is about Christ, not about us." I've searched the Scriptures from Genesis to Revelation and there is not one verse that even implies such a misconception. This is a man-made teaching that is necessary to support contrived doctrines. Ideas like this come up because Western thought is often filtered through a Grecian lens. These thought processes are shaped by the Greeks' numerous false gods who glowered over lowly subjects. This is the truth spoken in Jesus own words: "The Sabbath was made for man, not man for the Sabbath."[3]

Indeed, our God of love came in person to walk among us and to serve.[4] Now we serve a loving, merciful, long-suffering, redeeming God who makes binding covenants with those called by His name. He bonds with us in a covenant of love. The Lord Almighty, whom we serve, is a relational Father who beckons us to come into His rest. He beckons us to dwell in His sheltering place. He calls for us to stand in His counsel.[5] His Son is our Bridegroom who is preparing a place for us to dwell with Him forever. He yearns for us to lift up holy hands into the heavenly realm to worship, serve, and minister in the living presence of Yeshua our High Priest, who serves in heaven's sanctuary.

Those who are in covenant with Christ are inseparable. God's people enter into His Most Holy presence by faith in Jesus Christ. They are covered in the righteousness of Jesus Christ and made one with Him in body, soul, and spirit. So, how is it possible to even think that our salvation is about Christ and not about us? Yes, our Lord Jesus alone made our salvation possible by the selfless, obedient sacrifice of His body and shedding of His blood on our behalf, for the forgiveness of our sins. He died for the sins of the world—a world full of people whom he desires to restore to sweet fellowship with their Creator. Christ's love fills us with a desire for inseparable fellowship.

God is faithful, who has called you into fellowship with his Son, Jesus Christ our Lord.

(1 Corinthians 1:9)

When God's people come together as one and then function in unison as working parts of the body of Christ, the world around them takes note. But infighting and pointing fingers are also noteworthy and give the Church's distractors ammunition to use against us. We divide Christ and His Church when we say to other Christians, "You can't worship with us because you do it all wrong." These divisive words take away our ability to function as one with Christ and His body.

---

3. Mark 2:27.
4. Matthew 20:28.
5. Psalm 73:24.

We are admonished to put aside selfish ambitions, repent of personal agendas, reform our set-in-stone paradigms and come together to serve. This is what the many parts of the body do when they are one in Christ. We come together in a unity of faith and lift up the cross of Jesus Christ, and the world around us comes to see that we serve a living Savior who is actively present with us to minister among His people. Those who are steeped in darkness will see the Light of Life shining out to offer hope. This earth-shattering miracle is possible because of Christ in us. In Him we submit ourselves to full fellowship in His body, the Church.

> *I in them and you in me—so that they may be brought to complete unity. Then the world will know that you sent me and have loved them even as you have loved me.*

(John 17:23)

Our God is worthy to be exalted above all the heavens and earth. The Almighty and Holy One is our King who dwells in all splendor and majesty. We lift up holy hands in praise to Yahweh, our God, who dwells in His sanctuary in the highest heavens and in the hearts of His people. As we gather together in our assemblies for worship, we sing out with wisdom's song, rejoicing in God who Created the heavens and the earth.[6] The High and Lofty One is our heavenly Father who is worthy of all praise. He delights in His people and "crowns the humble with salvation."[7] He gathers together all those who are contrite of heart to make them one in the fellowship of His Son.

The Lord of Hosts lifts up the meek who are crushed in a world of darkness. By the power of His Word and the Holy Spirit, He reveals our sin and our need of Christ. He brings our hearts to repentance. He is always faithful and just to forgive us our sins and to cleanse us of even the stain of sin. Our Lord and God makes us new creations in Christ. We become His children of faith as we hear and receive the words of eternal life. The waters of baptism make us one in Christ in His suffering, death, burial, and resurrection. The Spirit of Grace breathes life into us and brings us into the sweet fellowship of the saints in His Church.

What an awesome God we serve.

> *For this is what the high and exalted One says—he who lives forever, whose name is holy: "I live in a high and holy place, but also with the one who is contrite and lowly in spirit, to revive the spirit of the lowly and to revive the heart of the contrite."*

(Isaiah 57:15)

---

6. Psalm 149:1
7. Psalm 149:4

Before Christ Jesus fulfilled the Law, the Torah regulated all worship and nearly every aspect of daily life. God's commands guided the planting of fields, crop rotation, and methods for harvest. The Old Covenant established dietary rules and laws of commerce. The gates of Jerusalem opened and closed according to the Torah's prescribed times. But in reality, the Law condemned the people because its perfect standard was impossible for any mortal. Indeed, the Law shows us our need of Christ who perfectly fulfilled the Law.

Because of Jesus' vicarious suffering and death on the cross, we are no longer under the curse of the Law. Its decrees can no longer condemn us to death because the resurrected Christ redeemed us and indwells us. Now we are called to dwell in fullness of our Lord and Savior; in His victorious death, burial, and resurrection. Jesus fulfilled every aspect of the Old Testament requirements and set us free from sin's grip, from Satan and death so that we may produce the fruits of the Spirit—the bounty of the true Vine.

> *So, my brothers and sisters, you also died to the law through the body of Christ, that you might belong to another, to him who was raised from the dead, in order that we might bear fruit for God.*
>
> (Romans 7:4)

Modern day Christians who grew up going to Sunday School learned about Jesus who lives in their hearts. Today's people of faith have a sense of Christ who takes up residence in them. What we often overlook is that we are called, in turn, to abide in Christ. When we are baptized into Christ and His death, burial, and resurrection we are made a working part in the body of Christ. We are called to enter a union with Christ and all working parts of His body, the Church.

Sons and daughters of the Most High God who are called by His holy name are beckoned to persevere, live in keeping with repentance, and in accord with their baptism. Our faithfulness is important because that is how healthy parts of the body function. Continual departures from faith and willful yielding of ourselves to the temptations of sin can turn us into a cancer that affects the whole body. If we refuse discipline and persist in deviant behavior, we lose the sweet fellowship we have come to enjoy with our heavenly Father. To remain in Christ, we cannot linger where unrighteousness reigns.

> *Do you not know that your bodies are members of Christ himself? Shall I then take the members of Christ and unite them with a prostitute? Never!*
>
> (1 Corinthians 6:15)

We have the greatest possible hope because of Yeshua, our Savior, who indwells us. This assurance is a great mystery of the gospel; a puzzle worth the effort to put together so we can see Christ in all His glory. We dig in the Scriptures so that we may grow in grace and knowledge. God's Word shapes our lives as we discover pearls of wisdom and receive treasures of the kingdom of heaven.[8] This everlasting hope offers a solid foundation for us to build our lives upon as we prepare for our returning Bridegroom.

The Law that Moses gave to the tribes of Israel revealed Christ their Messiah. Prescribed forms of worship and required pilgrimages to joyful feasts at the temple in Jerusalem cast a shadow of their Deliverer. Now, by means of the cross, we have the reality of Christ who indwells us so we may joyfully feast upon our Lord and Savior. The Spirit of Christ keeps us safe until the day when Christ, our Messiah, is fully revealed.

> *To them God has chosen to make known among the Gentiles the glorious riches of this mystery, which is Christ in you, the hope of glory.*

(Colossians 1:27)

The Spirit of Life breathed into us a need for fellowship. It's easy to think that the Almighty didn't need the man He created. Did His acts of creation require man's help? But Yahweh loved Adam and because of this bond of fellowship He brought him into the work of creation. The Lord brought all the animals and birds He formed out of the ground to see what Adam would call them. God could have named all the animals without Adam's help. But He is a God of covenantal relationships. Because of His love for Adam, He brought him into the work of creation to name the wild beasts and the birds of the air.

God's affinity for fellowship becomes evident when He formed Eve out of Adam's rib. It was not until Eve came to stand beside Adam that the Creator looked upon all He had made and saw that it as "very good."[9] Then the Lord walked with the first couple in the garden each day as the evening breeze wafted through Eden. Indeed, He created them for fellowship and with a need for fellowship. They came together every day as family to enjoy sweet communion; to walk, talk, and laugh. Certainly, it was as if they frolicked together as they enjoyed the variety of colors and the wind-borne fragrances of Eden's Garden.

The Creator's nature has not changed. As Christians we are baptized into His only Son, Jesus Christ, who indwells us. But it's not a one-sided relationship. We have a covenant of fellowship. God's sons and daughters are

---

8. See author's book, *Treasures of the Kingdom*.
9. Genesis 1:31.

called to abide in Christ and His body, the Church. Together we take part in a sweetness of community. We are called to an active relationship with the Father, Son, and Holy Spirit, and an equally important communion with our brothers and sisters in a gathering of faith. Love compels us to enjoy daily fellowship that is a vital part of our relational and covenantal communion.

Chapter 5

Created for Fellowship

Q & A

1. What is the connection between loving someone and needing them?

2. Describe God's covenant of love and its effect on our worship, acts of service, and our daily lives.

3. What purpose does the Old Testament Law serve today?

4. Why did the Creator bring Adam into the work of creation?

My Journal Notes:

United in our Gatherings

Key Scriptures:

- "He will also keep you firm to the end, so that you will be blameless on the day of our Lord Jesus Christ. God is faithful, who has called you into fellowship with his Son, Jesus Christ our Lord." (1 Corinthians 1:8–9)
- "But if we walk in the light, as he is in the light, we have fellowship with one another, and the blood of Jesus, his Son, purifies us from all sin." (1 John 1:7)

It's an inescapable truth that the world around us was designed with fellowship in mind. The core of all social structures reflects the Creator's desire. He established the foundations for families, churches, civic organizations, and communities that serve to bring us together. This lesson portrays this truth, showing today's disciples as a united fellowship in Jesus' holy name.

This topic gets personal, showing us how failures in our fellowship with Christ affect the whole body of faith. The learner is challenged to see themselves united with Jesus in fellowship, entering into His suffering, death, and resurrection. We'll learn how devastating it is when there's a cog missing in the gears. What happens when parts don't mesh together to work as designed? The whole mechanism requires all the parts be untarnished, mended, well-oiled, and joined together.

We'll learn that love is the glue, the mortar that holds all this together. The light of Word of creation serves to drive back the darkness that attempts to drive us away from unity among the sheep of God's pasture.

Study Prayer:

Heavenly Father, may we read your word all the days of our lives so that we may learn to revere you and follow carefully all your teachings.

A prayer according to Deuteronomy 17:19

John became known as the Apostle of Love. The fellowship of the saints is an important part of his message, inspired by his love and passion for Christ. He knew that disciples cannot be united with Christ if they constantly choose to isolate themselves from gatherings for fellowship, worship, ministry, and service in the presence of Christ our High Priest. Our love for our Savior is the catalyst for this fellowship. Love is exercised and strengthened as we gather together in Jesus' holy name. In our worship assemblies we bask in the light of Christ who strengthens us. In the fellowship of the congregation we are armored up for the battles we'll face in the days ahead.

This loving, caring fellowship is much more than just giving up an hour of sleep-in time to go sit in a row of chairs, sing along, and then meditate with our eyes closed while we endure a long sermon. What it really means is sacrificing ourselves, our time, our energy, and our resources to bond together with other people of faith. We must invest ourselves in the lives of others who come together in sweet fellowship in Jesus' name.

> *If we claim to have fellowship with him and yet walk in the darkness, we lie and do not live out the truth.*

(1 John 1:6)

Peter begins his first epistle with a powerful statement of truth. Let's consider his words that teach us about being united in Christ. In his letter to God's elect people, he states that, from the beginning, the Creator knew whom He has chosen to be called His sons and daughters. Then Peter teaches us that it is the work of the Spirit of Grace to sanctify us. Now look at the core truth of his opening message. God's elect are chosen to be obedient to Christ. The Apostle Paul teaches this same truth, encouraging the elect to be "conformed to the image of His Son."[1]

Our personal obedience affects the fellowship of the whole body of Christ. The wrong we do with our hands, the vile words we speak with our mouths, and the hostilities we inflict on the people around us brings shame upon the name of our Lord. It also interferes with the proper functioning of all who fellowship with us. Our sin makes us like a missing cog in the gear that causes a working machine to grind to a halt.

> *To God's elect, exiles scattered throughout the provinces of Pontus, Galatia, Cappadocia, Asia and Bithynia, who have been chosen according to the foreknowledge of God the Father, through the sanctifying work of the Spirit, to be obedient to Jesus Christ and sprinkled with his blood: Grace and peace be yours in abundance.*

(1 Peter 1:1–2)

---

1. Romans 8:29.

Consider the fellowship of the Church in this light. Each one of us is a working part of the body of Christ, the Church. Now think about the human body. Everybody has many functioning body parts that work together. When one part of our body stops working properly, medical treatment is required. When a muscle in our back doesn't function just right, we have to go to physical therapy and the treatment can be painful at first. If our appendix malfunctions, we might try some home remedies. If that doesn't work, we'll get a prescription for antibiotics. But the final treatment is surgical removal of our appendix.

God's chosen people are called to serve as working parts of the body in obedience to Christ. If we stop functioning according to our purpose, we are disciplined, and this discipline can be painful. We are called to repentance and to turn from our wayward ways. When we willingly continue in rebellion we become like a cancer in the body of Christ and it must be removed. Unless we repent, we are in danger of hearing those dreadful words: "I never knew you."[2] But there is great hope as we remain one in fellowship with Christ. We are forgiven and cleansed so we may be obedient—overcomers who serve as fully-functioning parts of the whole body of Christ.

> *For just as the body is one and has many members, and all the members of the body, though many, are one body, so it is with Christ. For in one Spirit we were all baptized into one body–Jews or Greeks, slaves or free–and all were made to drink of one Spirit.*

(1 Corinthians 12:12–13 ESV)

Walking in agreement with Christ's holy presence is the key to being compatible with Christ who indwells us. Our body is a temple where the Holy Spirit dwells and it must be kept clean through repentance and the cleansing fire of the Spirit. Are we required to keep every commandment perfectly so that Christ may come to indwell us? Is it necessary to be that perfect child to continue abiding in Him? Perfection is impossible for fallible beings. But we are called to enter into Christ Jesus in His perfection. Now that we have been baptized into Christ, His suffering, death and resurrection, our hearts well up with a desire to walk in the light of Christ, conformed to Christ and living our daily lives as if walking in Jesus' footsteps.

For those who abide in Christ there is no place for "fire" of our own making.[3] Our strength and confidence come by means of the Word and the Spirit of Christ. His fire flames out from our spirit and soul so the world around us will see Christ in us. The burning fire of the indwelling Spirit assures us of our Lord's eternal promise that He is preparing a place for us to live with Him forever. Our own fire burns out, while the fire of the Holy Spirit burns forever.

---
2. Matthew 7:23.
3. Isaiah 50:11.

The one who keeps God's commands lives in him, and he in them. And this is how we know that he lives in us: We know it by the Spirit he gave us.

(1 John 3:24)

A day is coming when we will see our heavenly Father face to face.[4] Right now, today, we are the face of Christ to the world around us. We are the love of Christ shown to imperfect and sometimes impossible people who gather with us to worship in Jesus' holy name. We're taught to welcome and love the weak, the needy, and even wandering souls. This overflow of care and love for our neighbors is the fruit produced by those who abide in Christ and His love.

We look forward to seeing God in all His glory, but even today He reveals Himself to us. We can know His nature. It's possible to know the desires of His heart. Those who seek may know the mysteries of the Gospel. Then, in wisdom and knowledge, and by the power of the word and the Holy Spirit, we speak out what He is speaking. He speaks out His tender and loving words through us to bring healing to wounded souls He brings into our lives. A touch of our hands in Jesus' name is His touch to heal the broken-hearted we see around us at every turn of life. This is the effect of His real, true, and perfect love overflowing from the throne of Grace through His servants.

No one has ever seen God; but if we love one another, God lives in us and his love is made complete in us.

(1 John 4:12)

People who are visually-impaired can be exceptionally enlightened in Christ. Quite often they see the light of truth better than people whose vision gets distracted by the world's eye candy. This fact makes it obvious that Jesus' teaching refers to the eyes of our spirit. If our eyes are dimmed because of rebellion in our hearts, our soul and spirit will be masked in the shadows of night. Seditious hearts like to think they have plenty of light, but their light is nothing more than wisps of smoke from a snuffed-out candle.

Now consider the ministries of Jesus as He walked among us as Immanuel, God With Us. He gave hope to the blind. He restored their sight so they could see the light of day. Every one of Jesus' sight-giving miracles serves to enlighten us to the power of His name that restores sight to the spiritually blind.

O Lord, open our eyes that we may see you in all your glory.

---

4. 1 Corinthians 13:12.

But if your eyes are unhealthy, your whole body will be full of darkness. If then the light within you is darkness, how great is that darkness!

(Matthew 6:23)

It's important to remind ourselves of a foundational truth. The Word of Creation spoke before time began, saying: "Let there be light." In an instant, the battle lines were drawn between light and darkness. Now, in the power of the Spirit, we armor up to join the battle, pressing forward to take the offensive. We press forward and wield the sword of the Spirit, that is the word of God. The Apostle Paul wrote powerful words to encourage us in battle: "The night is nearly over; the day is almost here. So let us put aside the deeds of darkness and put on the armor of light."[5]

Too often we are like soldiers who run from the battle and hide in a cave called Denial. But today is our day to come into the light. Take the sword of the Spirit in one hand and a torch with the light of Christ in the other. Shoulder to shoulder, we march out and sing out with our once downtrodden brothers and sisters, "We shall overcome!"

The light shines in the darkness, and the darkness has not overcome it.

(John 1:5)

Who can we trust? Bold news headlines shout out with distressing proclamations of environmental calamities that lurk on every mountain, forest, and valley. We're running out of water. Warming oceans create killer storms. We live in dread of drought-caused wildfires that might threaten our homes. What are we getting out of wallowing in dark headlines and filling our children with fear and despair?

The reality is that people love darkness more than light. Because of this, we continue to defile God's creation with our sin. Our deviant ways encourage the forces of destruction and the creeping darkness of night.[6] It's easier to worry about carbon footprints than to repent of our sin. We flounder in life's distresses and reject the Light of Life because His light reveals our sin. We prefer to lurk in dark shadows to conceal our violent ways.[7]

We can no longer sit on the fence. Will we wallow in the kingdom of darkness or bask in the kingdom of light? If we continue to walk in darkness will our deeds remain hidden? Or is it better to step into the light where our sin becomes obvious so that we may repent?

---

5. Romans 13:12.
6. Isaiah 24:5, Joel 2:3.
7. Psalm 139:1–12.

> *This is the verdict: Light has come into the world, but people loved darkness instead of light because their deeds were evil.*

(John 3:19)

A self-made person fashions an image of themselves from the stone salvaged from earth's rubble. Rock chips fly with each strike of the mallet. They keep chiseling away and finally their stone likeness materializes—an image of their own making. With each calculated strike, their likeness emerges and locks them into serving what they created—an idol their own hands crafted.

This is the image we leave for our children. We told our daughters and sons they could be whatever they wanted. We gave them no foundation to build their lives on. Before long our adult children realized that what their parents handed down offers no hope. Boomers built a culture that revels in the idolatry of self. Everyone scrambles for their moment in the limelight—a few moments of fame. But the heart and soul of a whole generation ends up feeling empty and betrayed.

Chiseled stone cannot speak life-giving words. In our times of trouble, our rock-hewn image erodes, crumbles, and creates more rubble. Self-made people have nothing but a false hope. The end is devastation when this stone likeness falls and crushes its maker.

> *The "gods" know nothing, they understand nothing. They walk about in darkness; all the foundations of the earth are shaken.*

(Psalm 82:5)

Meet Yegor Grownsley, a farmer wannabe. Observe as he waddles in his rubber boots on his way to study his corn patch for the umpteenth time to see if his corn started to grow. But he only finds weeds. He stands there in his worn denim bib overalls with his fingers buried in his thick, wavy hair. He scratches his grey matter like he's trying to get his brain in gear. He kicks at the weeds in disgust and turns around, unexpectedly facing his pesky neighbor.

"What's happening, Yegor? No corn yet?" He chuckles.

"Not a single corn sprout, you see. Musta got bad seed." Yegor points with disgust at the weeds growing in the corn rows.

Mr. Pesky stoops over to pull a seed packet off its stake at the end of the row. "Did you follow the directions?"

"Don't need that. I been thinking 'bout garden stuff all winter long. I know what I'm doing here."

Yegor's persistent neighbor taps his finger on the back of the seed packet. "Says here to plant the corn after danger of frost is past. But you planted six weeks ago in February."

This short dialogue helps us see that the principles of growing corn can also apply to our call to persevere in our faith. We have the Bible's instructions to follow so that we can bear good fruit. It's not a matter of "must do this," and "must not do that." Instead, those who are brought to saving faith, forgiven, and cleansed come to love their Savior so much that they dig in to learn Scripture's imperatives so they can walk according to the great love planted in their hearts. Like a gardener who works in agreement with nature, Jesus' disciples do their best work when they serve in agreement with the Bible's teaching.

We stand in a position of abundant blessings when we remain in Christ. Our Savior covers us like a grape arbor that flourishes with lavish fruitfulness. But all too often, fallible people prefer to walk in the dark because light works like a laser beam to expose unfaithfulness. But there is no fellowship with the Father if we remain in darkness.

> *Justice is far from us, and righteousness does not reach us. We look for light, but all is darkness; for brightness, but we walk in deep shadows.*

(Isaiah 59:9)

We serve an awesome God. He is faithful to hold us close to His heart, to keep us safe, united in fellowship, and blameless to the end of our days. By the power of His word and the Holy Spirit, He lights our pathway so that we may walk in the light of sweet fellowship. If we repeatedly choose to spiritually isolate, we deny ourselves the blessings of fellowship. Isolation goes against the nature of new creations in Christ. We can't be a working part of the body of Christ apart from our Savior. When we cut ourselves off from serving together, without input or output, we are in danger of putrefying. We may become like cancer in the body.

There is a better way. We are called to conform ourselves to Christ in a fellowship of faith. This means that we live in agreement with Jesus' holy indwelling presence. That day will come when we will see Him face to face. As we wait with our feet still planted here on planet Earth, we serve as the face of Christ to our family, friends, and neighbors.

For us to grow in love and fellowship we need good spiritual eyes. Do you feel like your eyes are dim? Take heart because Jesus restores sight to the spiritually blind. Now that our eyes are opened to the light of Christ, we are called to put on the armor of light, take up the sword of the Spirit, and lift up the light of Christ to drive back darkness in the world around us. As soldiers of light, we can't let ourselves be distracted by the cares of a fallen world. We're fallible beings who find it easier to worry about carbon footprints than to confess sin that defiles God's creation. The best environmental solution is to build our lives on a solid foundation; the Rock who is our Redeemer. People who chisel out their own image from earth's stone have no foundation to build their lives on. They end up empty and betrayed.

We are called to step into the light so that we may be united with Christ in sweet fellowship with all people of saving faith. Together we are like branches grafted into the Vine, encouraging each other to bear good fruit. Because of our love for Christ, we follow the Bible's instructions so that our gardens blossom and flourish with the good fruit of fellowship.

Chapter 6

United in our Gatherings

Q & A

1. What is the catalyst for Christian fellowship?

   _____
   _____
   _____

2. How does one person's disobedience or obedience affect the whole church?

   _____
   _____
   _____

3. Why does a self-made person end up without a solid foundation for building their lives?

   _____
   _____
   _____

4. Why do people avoid the light of Christ?

   _____
   _____
   _____

My Journal Notes:

Partakers of the Bread of Life

Key Scripture:

- "Very truly I tell you, the one who believes has eternal life. I am the bread of life. Your ancestors ate the manna in the wilderness, yet they died. But here is the bread that comes down from heaven, which anyone may eat and not die. I am the living bread that came down from heaven. Whoever eats this bread will live forever. This bread is my flesh, which I will give for the life of the world. Very truly I tell you, unless you eat the flesh of the Son of Man and drink his blood, you have no life in you. Whoever eats my flesh and drinks my blood has eternal life, and I will raise them up at the last day. For my flesh is real food and my blood is real drink. Whoever eats my flesh and drinks my blood remains in me, and I in them. Just as the living Father sent me and I live because of the Father, so the one who feeds on me will live because of me. This is the bread that came down from heaven. Your ancestors ate manna and died, but whoever feeds on this bread will live forever." (John 6:47–58)

Gathering family and friends around a table filled with a cornucopia of roasted meats, salads, and sweets is an incredible bonding experience. When Christians gather in Jesus' name, they are bound together as one in Christ at the Lord's Table. We partake of Christ at His table; the bread and the cup of communion. Jesus instituted this remembrance as He celebrated the Passover meal with His disciples after sunset on the 14th day of Nisan.[1] Now, when we come to the Lord's Table, we enter the holy presence of the Spirit of Christ. This is a high and holy place where Jesus our High Priest ministers forgiveness and strengthens the saints. In this study, we'll search Old and New Testament teaching about gathering together at the Lord's Table. A complete perspective is important to bring us into the light of Christ's blessings that are ours at this blessed table.

---

1. Matthew 26:17.

> Study Prayer:
>
> *O Bread of Life, teach us to do your will, for you are our God; may your good Spirit lead us on level ground.*
>
> A prayer according to Psalm 143:10

Malachi serves as our first teacher in this session. He admonishes God's people for showing contempt when coming to the Lord's Table. They offered crippled and diseased animals when an unblemished sacrifice was required as they came to feast before the Lord. The prophet goes on to lament their scornful worship because of their unworthy offerings for Yahweh's altar. Malachi calls for someone to shut the temple doors to keep out self-serving worshippers who come with unacceptable sacrifices.

> "Oh, that one of you would shut the temple doors, so that you would not light useless fires on my altar! I am not pleased with you," says the Lord Almighty, "and I will accept no offering from your hands."

(Malachi 1:10)

Malachi's lament brings to mind the account of Cain's wrongheaded sacrifice in Genesis. Cain came self-confident and foolish to sacrifice before the Almighty. Rather than bringing a blood sacrifice to the altar and presenting an offering according to truth and righteousness, he brought crops from his own field. Neither vegetables nor fig leaves can serve as a covering for sin.[2] Because of this egregious offense, the Lord would not accept his sacrifice. The consequences were severe. This ought to perk up our ears to listen and learn what our Lord desires of us when we come to partake of Christ.

Because God is holy, the Apostle Paul admonishes us to examine ourselves before we come to the Lord's Table. This is a holy place and we come into Christ's presence with reverence and awe because of what God has done for us. At the communion table, we enter into forgiveness and the Spirit's cleansing. We must not come complacent or with contempt. We come with disdain if we gather around the Lord's Table with an attitude of, "Here I am, Lord. What you see is what you get."

Arrogant ignorance denies our own sin and the power of His blood that was shed for our forgiveness and cleansing of our sinful condition. A self-confident and foolish attitude leads to complacency. We must not be cavalier about the effectiveness of Jesus' blood shed for the remission of our sins. At

---

2. Genesis 3:7.

this holy table we come to be washed in His blood from the inside out. When we partake of Christ's body and blood, we enter into His holy presence. No lesser sacrifice will do. We come fully aware of our sinful condition, offering ourselves as a living sacrifice, to be washed and made acceptable before Christ Jesus our High Priest.[3]

> *Examine yourselves to see whether you are in the faith; test yourselves. Do you not realize that Christ Jesus is in you–unless, of course, you fail the test?*

(2 Corinthians 13:5)

We come to the Lord's Table as fallible beings with contrite hearts. At this bountiful table, imperfect believers are forgiven and made holy and acceptable as living sacrifices. We present ourselves before our ministering High Priest, Jesus Christ, as a declaration of faith, proclaiming that He indwells us and we are in Him.

What does it mean when Jesus takes up residence in us? It means that He inhabits every part of our body, soul, and spirit. In essence, we are dead to self and made alive in Christ. Our old way of doing things, our crude language, and our self-serving ways are all crucified with Christ and we are no longer subject to these forces of darkness.

In Christ we are made holy. We are separated to Him so we may live a life conformed to our Savior. We are molded and shaped into useful vessels, cleansed and set apart to worship in spirit and truth. A lifestyle of praise and thanksgiving begins with the first blink of our eyes in the morning, affects every word spoken and the work of our hands, and then we rest in His presence through the night hours. Indeed, we are living, active, pneumatized[4] sacrifices who bask in the eternal light of redemption. The light of Christ empowers us to worship from our spirit in accord with all that is true and right.

> *Therefore, I urge you, brothers and sisters, in view of God's mercy, to offer your bodies as a living sacrifice, holy and pleasing to God–this is your true and proper worship.*

(Romans 12:1)

Imagine hiking down a long wilderness trail and turning at a fork in the path that leads you through a desert wasteland. The hike is way longer than expected, and after a few days of being assaulted by cactus needles and prickly pear, both you, your friend, and your dog drink your last drops of water and taste the last crumbs of trail mix. You're out in the middle of nowhere

---

3. Ecclesiastes 5:1.
4. "Pneumatized," as used in this study, is the wind of the Holy Spirit breathed into our body, soul, and spirit that fills us.

and there's no sign of life except the howl of a coyote, the scurry of lizards, and the occasional flight of a cactus wren.

You snuggle down into your sleeping bag for the night with your stomach growling and your mouth as dry as the dust on your boots. But when the first light of dawn breaks over the horizon, you open your eyes just a peep and see bread on the rock by the cold ashes of your fire pit. Your dog is lapping from a small pool of fresh water just a few steps away.

The Apostle John recorded Jesus' words as He taught the people, showing them that He, Yeshua, was the miracle of manna from heaven and water from the rock that sustained the tribes of Israel as they wandered in the wilderness. Our Lord and Savior is the very Bread of Life, and He dwells in us as Provider of our daily bread. Jesus is the Wellspring of Life and He inhabits us in the fullness of His being. It is for us to remain in Him, partake of Him, and bask in the full blessings of His awesome presence.

> *For the bread of God is the bread that comes down from heaven and gives life to the world. "Sir," they said, "always give us this bread." Then Jesus declared, "I am the bread of life. Whoever comes to me will never go hungry, and whoever believes in me will never be thirsty."*

(John 6:33–35)

Do you want to live your life to the fullest? Then toss out the bucket list you made up and live in the light of Christ. We are called to live as partakers of Christ, nourished by His word and strengthened as we feed on the Bread of Life. Do you have a desire for real, satisfying spiritual food that sustains your eternal soul and spirit? Then come again and again to the Lord's Table and feed on the Bread of Life and drink from the cup of His shed blood. The bread and the cup of communion offer security in Christ. We remain shielded by our Savior's right hand as we partake of Him who indwells us.

> *You make known to me the path of life, you will fill me with joy in your presence, with eternal pleasures at your right hand.*

(Psalm 16:11)

Thanksgiving is the favorite holiday for many people. It's a time when family and friends gather around a bountiful table with thankful hearts to feast before God who Provides.[5] It's a great time for renewing bonds of fellowship and friendship in a plentiful gathering. But this is a mere shadow of an even greater supper.

---

5. Philippians 4:19.

The power, effect, and blessings of gathering around the Lord's Table in Jesus' name are beyond words to describe. This table has a unifying effect, bonding us together as one in Christ. Every element of Christ is ours as we partake of Him at His table. We are made acceptable living sacrifices before Jesus, our High Priest, as we partake of the bread and cup of communion. Before Christians come to this table, we are called to examine themselves to be sure that we are truly in the faith.[6]

All those who are called by the name of Yeshua, our Lord and Savior, come together at the Lord's Table to share the bread and cup, and there He inhabits us and strengthens our fellowship in Him. Every part of our body, soul, and spirit are saturated with Christ.[7] Jesus is the Bread of Life who indwells us in the fullness of His being. He is peace, comfort, joy, strength, love, faithfulness, and so much more than all we could ask or imagine. And His holy presence indwells us in all His majesty.

The Bread of Life and the cup of Jesus' blood secure us in Christ. Indeed, these elements administered in Jesus' presence are Christ in us. The bread we receive in our hand and the cup we drink are visible manifestations of Christ Jesus. With His nail-scarred hands He offers His broken body and shed blood, the elements of a New Covenant ministered to us in heaven's sanctuary.[8]

---

6. 1 Corinthians 11:27–29.
7. 2 Peter 1:3–4.
8. Hebrews 8:1-2.

Chapter 7

Partakers of the Bread of Life

Q & A

1. What can we learn from Cain's unacceptable sacrifice?

2. Why must Christians come to the Lord's Table to partake of the bread and the cup?

3. Where can you find real, satisfying spiritual food that sustains your eternal soul and spirit?

4. Why must we examine ourselves before coming to the Lord's Table?

My Journal Notes:

Games We Play with Darkness

Key Scriptures:

- "You are a chosen people, a royal priesthood, a holy nation, God's special possession, that you may declare the praises of him who called you out of darkness into his wonderful light." (1 Peter 2:9)

- "This is the message we have heard from him and declare to you: God is light; in him there is no darkness at all. If we claim to have fellowship with him and yet walk in the darkness, we lie and do not live out the truth. But if we walk in the light, as he is in the light, we have fellowship with one another, and the blood of Jesus, his Son, purifies us from all sin."
(1 John 1:5–7)

Mancala is among the world's oldest games still played today. This strategy game uses small stones, beans, or seeds on a board with small holes. The object is to capture an opponent's game pieces. Throughout time, many games have been invented and we all have our favorites. When children are left alone, they make up their own games using sticks and stones if that's all they have. A little box of cards can provide a nice diversion on a stormy weekend when we're snowed in. There are too many game choices and it's always best to apply godly wisdom when we choose. When pastimes are flooded with light and life, they are refreshing diversions from the daily grind. This study offers us an opportunity to examine ourselves by checking out the games in our closet, and taking account of the games we play.

Stories told about Israel's wars of independence include reports of warriors who observed unwritten rules about hours of battle. They fought to defend themselves during daylight and then after dark they often got together to eat and play card games with the men who had been shooting at them. While this may be okay on some battlefields, this doesn't work for soldiers of the light. You can't put up a good front in the daylight, and then play games with darkness when the shadows grow long and the sun slides beneath the horizon.

The Word of Creation spoke light to shine out and pierce the darkness.[1] The light that beamed out on day one of creation continues to shine brighter and brighter until our victorious Messiah, the Light of the World, is fully revealed. We are called to separate ourselves from the dark side of life, put on the armor of light, and press forward toward Christ's great and final victory. The Scriptures in this study teach us to throw off the games we play that hinder us in our walk of faith.[2]

> Study Prayer:
>
> *O Lord who alone is holy,*
> *make your face shine on your servants and teach us your decrees.*
>
> A prayer according to Psalm 119:135

The Apostle Paul asks a pertinent question: "What fellowship can light have with darkness?"[3] This struggle rages between our flesh and spirit and it's amplified in the culture around us. Everything from death metal to advertising campaigns attempt to mold us in their image, often in conflict with truth and light of the kingdom of heaven. But we are called to be a people set apart to Christ, kept from works of darkness, and to defend all justice and righteousness.[4]

> *For our struggle is not against flesh and blood, but against the rulers, against the authorities, against the powers of this dark world and against the spiritual forces of evil in the heavenly realms.*
>
> (Ephesians 6:12)

The light of every sunrise radiates out with great hope as we look forward to the full revelation of Christ victorious. As the night skies grow dark, the moon rises on the horizon to light the night as God's faithful witness in the sky.[5] From the beginning of time, the stars shine to pierce through dark skies with brilliant points of light, displaying the wonders of God's creation. Then, after many sunrises and sunsets, a greater light entered the scene. The Light dawned for a people who lived in the shadow of death.[6] John the Baptizer announced the Light by saying: "Behold the Lamb of God who takes away the sin of the world."[7]

---

1. Genesis 1:2.
2. Hebrews 12:1.
3. 2 Corinthians 6:14.
4. Isaiah 56:1.
5. Psalm 89:37.
6. Matthew 4:16.
7. John 1:29.

We are called to armor up while there is still time to stand with Christ and serve as messengers of light. We proclaim God's Word that delivers lost souls who may be hardened by the deceitfulness of darkness.[8] With the sword of the Spirit gripped in our hands, we wield powerful words of grace to thwart forces that lurk in the night to prey on those who wander.

> *The night is nearly over; the day is almost here. So let us put aside the deeds of darkness and put on the armor of light.*

(Romans 13:12)

If you've ever been caught in a deep forest after the sun goes down, with no moonlight or flashlight, you know what it's like to stumble around in darkness. It's a frightening experience. Every snapping twig and rustling leaf makes you shudder with fear of what might be lurking unseen in the dark. The darkness caught you unaware. Your eyes dart about for some light to show the way back to your campsite. You'll have to wait for the light before you can return.

While you're standing with your feet tangled up and no clue which way to go, listen up and look up. Jesus, the Good Shepherd is calling out your name. The sound of His voice echoes with a resonance of compassionate love. He knows the dark pathway you've chosen for your life and He holds out His nail-scarred hands to you. He is the Light of the World who offers forgiveness and mercy.

> *When Jesus spoke again to the people, he said, "I am the light of the world. Whoever follows me will never walk in darkness, but will have the light of life."*

(John 8:12)

Dark, smoke-filled rooms serve as hidden recesses for those who engage in illicit gaming; a playtime no one can know about. A secret knock and password gain your entry. But this isn't the only place darkness has a stronghold. Open the doors of your game closet at home and turn on the light. Take an account of the games you play. How do the games inside the boxes on the shelf look in the light of truth and righteousness? Take an inventory of your pastime distractions, asking yourself: "Is this something that will stand true in the light of Christ?"

We all need fun diversions, especially games that we play together with family and friends. It makes for good times of fun, snacks, and laughter. It helps to have a game of solitaire on our cell phone to pass the time on a long flight. For those who are in Christ, the measure of a game's value is the holy

---

8. Hebrews 3:13.

Scriptures. We need to examine our hearts and ask; "When playing that game, does it shed light into this dark world, or does it feed my weaknesses? Do the games I play feed my habits or do they strengthen my spirit?"

> *Everyone who does evil hates the light, and will not come into the light for fear that their deeds will be exposed. But whoever lives by the truth comes into the light, so that it may be seen plainly that what they have done has been done in the sight of God.*

(John 3:20–21)

Proverbs chapter seven tells the story of a young man who goes out for an evening stroll and just happens along a street corner that has a bad reputation. He acts as if he's unaware of his surroundings, but as the light of day fades over the horizon his heart is drawn deeper into the secret desires of the night. He sees a young gal who claims to have fulfilled her vows before the Lord, acting as if she's a good person. But it's a false cover. Her ruby lips drip with deceptive words. She says, "Nobody will know. My husband is away on business."[9]

In modern terms this might be written: "She just got home from church and was reading a Bible on her front porch. She wore a glittering gold cross to grace her neckline." But entering through her front door is like stepping onto the highway to hell. It's easy to end up at this doorway. Too often we deceive ourselves, saying, "They're a good person. It's okay, we'll never get caught." But our sins cannot be hidden forever. We can be sure that, when morning light breaks over the horizon, our sins will be exposed.[10] We need to remind ourselves that walking according to the Spirit of Christ is a narrow path. Darkness lurks and tries to draw us to walk too close to the edge, drifting further and further from the pathway's light. One little compromise at a time makes our feet slip away. We try to pick ourselves up and dust off, but we're all tangled up and can't get ourselves free. Then in the moment of our distress the Good Shepherd comes looking for us. He came to rescue us, clean us up, draw us close, and bring us home with rejoicing.

> *He was going down the street near her corner, walking along in the direction of her house at twilight, as the day was fading, as the dark of night set in.*

(Proverbs 7:8–9)

What is the point of doing anything good? Why should we go out of our way to be a good Samaritan when those people created the mess they're in? There are problems that are too big for us to solve. Climate change causes

---
9. Proverbs 7:19.
10. Luke 12:2.

storms that destroy our safe towns and cities. Our leaders lie to us and the government is in chaos. There's a pandemic devastating us in waves. We've become a god-forsaken land, so why should we sweat the small stuff, and the big stuff is too overwhelming. Just leave us alone to play our little games in dark corners—no one will see us.

The darkness of violence and corruption comes over us like a swarm of Africanized bees. All the dangers confront God's people with a question. Will we remain in the shelter of the Most High God? Will we step out, armored up in His armor of light to drive back the darkness? Or will we play games in dark dungeons, attempting to hide what we do when no one can see us? We know the right answer. Let's come together and stand up to walk in the full light of day.[11]

> *He said to me, "Son of man, have you seen what the elders of Israel are doing in the darkness, each at the shrine of his own idol? They say, 'The Lord does not see us; the Lord has forsaken the land.'"*

(Ezekiel 8:12)

There are no secrets except in our imagination. What we do in the dark eventually gets exposed in the light. Too many parents think they're keeping bad habits well concealed, only to find one of their children caught in the same trap. It doesn't work to put on a mask in front of friends, family, and coworkers to hide the reality of who we are deep inside.[12]

What we do in the dark will not stay hidden forever. The light of Christ comes like the morning sun to expose dark deeds and show us our need of Christ as Lord and Savior. We're like a house that looks great inside when the lights are out, but open the blinds to the morning sun and suddenly all the dirt, dust, and clutter become obvious. The light of Christ serves to show us that we need a Redeemer to cleanse our lives and make us clean temples where the Lord may dwell.

> *You have set our iniquities before you, our secret sins in the light of your presence.*

(Psalm 90:8)

Can we descend into the indulgences of Sin City's valley and come away unscathed? Is it possible to partake in the delights of Fat Tuesday and then be okay because we give up chocolate for Lent? Does compartmentalizing our lives work; dancing and crooning to death metal on Saturday night and then singing some Christian songs on Sunday morning?

---

11. Proverbs 4:18.
12. Luke 11:39.

We know that willfully indulging ourselves in moments of illicit pleasure is not an unforgivable sin. But we must "rend our hearts"[13] and turn away from depravity and be cleansed of our duplicity. When temptations assault us, it's important to remember that forgiveness does not preclude consequences. There is a much better way than wandering on that broad easy pathway. We are called to walk in the light of a narrow path. The light of Christ drives back the darkness so we may stand together as a holy nation. The dark street corners in the night are illuminated as we hold up the light. It's our job to be the light of Christ that drives back the darkness of the world. But it's not our place to forcefully drag someone away from their dark pursuits. What we can do is protect those who the violent would violate. We restore what the thief stole from a victim, provide food for the hungry, and clothe those who shiver in the cold. We lift up those who are beaten down by the cares of this world. We defend the fatherless. Our love-driven efforts serve to expose the deeds of darkness and restore God's creation.

Have nothing to do with the fruitless deeds of darkness, but rather expose them.

(Ephesians 5:11)

What we do with our leisure time can make us better people or drag us down into a dark abyss. We might attempt to set one foot in the light of Christ and the other in dungeons of darkness, but it's not possible because we can never serve two masters.[14] Instead, Jesus' followers are called to put on the armor of light and serve as messengers of light in a dark world. The games we play, toying with darkness, will trip us up and entangle us. They have no place in our game closet or our lives.

But as fallible humans we tend to get ourselves ensnared, our feet slipping from Jesus' pathway. The glitter and glamor of the world looks so attractive, but the sparkle turns into brambles and thorns that trap us. It's too easy to get ourselves in a mess that we can't get ourselves out of. In our moments of hopelessness, we hear a voice, a Good Shepherd calling our name. He uses His shepherd's rod to set us free. Then He extends healing, forgiveness, and mercy to us in His nail-scarred hands. Even in hidden, smoke-filled rooms, He knows where we are and comes to set us free from the chains of our secret pursuits. We got caught up in our weaknesses, but now He reaches out to us to extend forgiveness and then strengthen us in all that is right and good. Yes, we can be sure that our Savior helps us and strengthens us even as we deal with the consequences of our sin.

---

13. Joel 2:13.
14. Matthew 6:24.

The world's temptations, at first glance, look so good and right. It's easy to justify ourselves to do the things we want. After all, she appears so innocent, sitting there reading her Bible. She just got home from church, right? And the guy who catches a girl's eye is wearing a cross around his neck, so he's okay, right? But we must not be deceived by those who claim to be so spiritual but then lead us through a doorway to ruin.

Our lives are constantly confronted with choices—moments that call for godly discernment. Will we play meaningless games in the dark, or will we put on the armor of light and be the light of the world that exposes deeds of darkness? We are called to serve as light, like the morning sun. This is the light of Christ that reveals the world's filth and clutter.

It's time to take account of ourselves and come out of the dungeons of darkness. Let us lift up the light of Christ and serve as the light of the world that drives out the darkness.

Chapter 8

Games we Play with Darkness

Q & A

1. Describe the battle between light and darkness that rages within each of us.

_____
_____
_____

2. What deceptive practices do pawns of darkness use to draw us into its dark games?

_____
_____
_____

3. Why is it so easy to get caught up in the games played in the darkness?

_____
_____
_____

4. Why should we go out of our way to do what is right and good when everyone else is enjoying the dark games in their closet?

_____
_____
_____

My Journal Notes:

Wandering from Home

Key Scriptures:

- "My brothers and sisters, if one of you should wander from the truth and someone should bring that person back, remember this: Whoever turns a sinner from the error of their way will save them from death and cover over a multitude of sins." (James 5:19–20)

- "You keep track of all my sorrows. You have collected all my tears in your bottle. You have recorded each one in your book." (Psalm 56:8 NLT)

Fallible mortal beings are prone to drift. Walking on a straight, well-lit path isn't enough for us. Our eyes tend to scan the horizon for greener pastures. In this study, we'll hear the perils of a wanderer who thought he could find a better life. His story helps us see how easily our hearts are tempted to search for an easier way. And why not? Everybody's getting rich and they all seem so carefree.[1]

It's too late when we finally learn it's all a trap, and we're caught in sin's deceptive snares. The glitter and gold are nothing but tinsel. It's all bait to capture us. We're like birds reduced to be one more prize locked away in a cage.[2] Our captors won't advocate for us after we're caught in their trap. They'll turn a deaf ear to our plea. But we are not left without hope. Our wandering ways will come to haunt us, but we have a Good Shepherd who hears every penitent cry. In this lesson we'll put our downfalls behind us and come into the loving arms of our Lord and Redeemer. He loves us, calls us by name, and comes to us with His comforting shepherd's rod to take us back into His fold.

Escalus instructs us in this study by sharing his misadventure. He serves as a fictional teacher in an imaginary village with a story to tell. Listen as he tells his tale to a short-term mission team shortly after they step ashore from their river boat.

---

1. Psalm 73:12.
2. Jeremiah 5:27.

> Study Prayer:
>
> *Good Shepherd, teach us your ways, so that we may walk in your paths.*
>
> A Prayer according to Isaiah 2:3

"Hello, hello to you friends. My name Escalus and I live all fifty and two year in my village. Welcome to Metslotania. Sorry, my Ingless so bad. I learn from missionary friend. Please, do you give time to hear story 'bout Jesus and me?

"When I were kid, I Christian, baptized and all. But you know, I young an cocky. Quit read my Bible and no more pray. Very bad time for me. I run away to big town but got big trouble on the way. Real bad night. I fall in big thorn bush. But I hear—not like people voice you know—but I hear my name call out. I know Jesus call me to go back home.

"Then I really close to Jesus again. We real, you know, what Ingless say, tight friend? I safe now. I like all church people now. It my new home where I stay. It so much good to me.

"No way to buy what I got now even if I empty all my pockets. No president, no rich man buy all that. See, I pull all out my pockets and one little copper coin, no more. But I have deal with my Jesus. He make me to belong, and He really like me. He wake me in morning like friend. He call me by name. Yeah, He really do that. He keep my heart full up with lots of thank you so I always sing praise song to Him. Jesus touch me to make me strong. So much love in my heart now. I go to church hungry for more Jesus and then I get full with good stuff from Bible. So good to be home with my Jesus.

"Look here verse I find in Bible 'bout that. But words here no Ingless, so I say Ingless for you."

> *The Lord like shepherd to me, I got what I need. He make to me sleep in green pasture, an take me to quiet water, he make fresh my soul. He show me along good path 'cause His name good.*

(Psalm 23:1–3)

"All be so very good for me when I kid, but then like fall off bike, hit my head an wander stupid. I think I be so strong so I go my away alone. Yeah, I know home people love, care 'bout me. I too, how you say, comfer, yes, comfort. I be like that sheep over on the hill in green grass. But big village on the other side of mountain better I think. So, what I do? I get up, go and sneak away at night time. Everything good for me at home—but not enough. Off I go wander like lost sheep. The big town over there sound so good I got to go see.

"The Bible know my story. It right here in Bible! I say it Ingless to you."

When I feed them, they satisfy; when they satisfy, then they proud, an forgot me.
(Hosea 13:6)

"You see little lambs flock on hill there? I have picture of Jesus hold them close to heart. But I be like sheep an run off when night get cold. Then find myself walk along and, how Ingless say, spooky it be so dark. That scaredy feeling bite at me like dog on my heel. I be like little sheep and leave safe home. I run away and feel like hard fist hold my heart. The dirt under my shoes no solid no more. Feel like slippy sand. Maybe quicken sand an it drag me down. Feel like go to be my grave. That path up mountain so dark. I always tripping over rock. Then fall down in thorny bush an I reach my hands to my home. My heart pound so hard. Home so far away. I yell and scream cause I caught in thorn bush. I try to be free but it grab on me. I call out but no people hear me. I never get out of mess I be in.

"Now I so happy, an Jesus say something 'bout that too."

Call on Jesus in very bad day; I come help you, an you honor me.
(Psalm 50:15)

"Big trouble for me, can breathe no more. I try an try to get out. Big problem for me in my stupid. Then I give up an feel weak like dirty raggedy. My run away idea drag me from safe home and now I got big trouble.

"I so sad an mad at me. I want give up. Then I think I hear calling my name. It so dark. So dark and I get cut bad, can't get out of thorns. My voice stop working. I try but cannot call for help to find me. I try to yell, but too weak, can't get out. My throat feel hurt from yell out. I try answer to my name but no voice. Dark feel like prison. I think 'bout song we sing of Jesus Shepherd. Where He be now? Will he come take me to home? I hear again, my name. Do I see light where it be so dark?

"I remember Jesus talk about my big trouble in Bible."

When walk through dark valley, fear no bad, for you with me; you have rod an shepherd stick to fix me okay again.
(Psalm 23:4)

"My shivers all over body. I afraid, so awful afraid. My throat so hurt I not breathing good. Do I hear again? Someone who know my name out in dark? Do I hear voice? I breathe out last wind to give up on me. Just slump down. No more strong.

"Then thorn bush move. My eyes so full of tears I don't see. Someone come to help? I know my God hear me cry. He get me out of tangle from bush of trouble. Yeah, I run off so proud and feel so strong, but now I know Jesus forgive my wander ways. He lift me up, clean me, and hold me so close I hear his heartbeat. Now I come to home 'cause Jesus help me—the Bible say so. This one hard for me in Ingless, so you read please."

> *The Spirit of the Lord is on me, because he has anointed me to proclaim good news to the poor. He has sent me to proclaim freedom for the prisoners and recovery of sight for the blind, to set the oppressed free, to proclaim the year of the Lord's favor.*

(Luke 4:18–19)

What did we learn from our new friend Escalus? His life experience teaches us that all those who are baptized into Christ are brought into the safety and security of the fold where the Good Shepherd keeps us secure in His love. The saints dwell in God's house where we lift up our voices to praise Him. But fallible humans have a wanderlust that leads them to drift away. In reality, we have it so good that we ought to do everything possible to stay under Christ's cover of protection. Instead, we become complacent and our eyes are drawn to the shallow glamour and affluence of those who wander down life's broad, easy path.

When we slip away from our Savior's presence, suddenly we are fraught with dread and anxiety that seems to come out of nowhere. We find ourselves caught in the thicket without light to show us the way out. We call out for help until our voice fails us. Caught up in our sin, we wonder if anyone hears us crying out in despair? It seems as if no one knows our plight and pain.

But there's a glimmer of hope upon hearing the Good Shepherd's voice. Jesus calls us by name. He hears our repentant plea. Our Savior frees us from the trappings of our sin, forgives us, and restores us with rejoicing because we're one lost lamb who is returned to the fold.

Have you wandered away? Are you far from enjoying His peaceful resting place in lush green pastures our Good Shepherd provides? Now is the time to cry out with repentance. He will hear you, pick you up, clean you up, restore you to the sweet fellowship of His presence, and give you a new song in your heart.

Blessed are those who dwell in your house; they are ever praising you.
(Psalm 84:4)

Welcome home, Escalus.

Chapter 9

Wandering from Home

Q & A

1. Why does grass always look greener on the other side of the mountain?

2. Why are people so willing to leave a place where they are safe and secure?

3. How can you be sure the Good Shepherd will answer your penitent cry for help?

4. Will the words in the Bible speak to us in the moment of personal trouble?

My Journal Notes:

Dressed and Ready

Key Scriptures:

- "Be dressed ready for service and keep your lamps burning, like servants waiting for their master to return from a wedding banquet, so that when he comes and knocks they can immediately open the door for him. It will be good for those servants whose master finds them watching when he comes. Truly I tell you, he will dress himself to serve, will have them recline at the table and will come and wait on them." (Luke 12:35–37)

- "The Lord answered, 'Who then is the faithful and wise manager, whom the master puts in charge of his servants to give them their food allowance at the proper time? It will be good for that servant whom the master finds doing so when he returns.'" (Luke 12:42–43)

Waiting in line at the Post Office can get us more worked up than a morning jog. Our running shoes can't stand still while we wait, listening to the person at the counter ask way too many questions about the pink envelope they're mailing to a granddaughter in Kansas. As we wait in line we have time to wonder; how did we get stuck in this hurry-up-and-wait world?

This study serves to instruct bridesmaids and bride as they get dressed for the great wedding banquet. There's a storm outside, so they must be clothed to protect themselves from sleet and hail. We'll learn to wait with a trusting expectation, not knowing the date or time of the Bridegroom's return. The following Scriptures encourage us to be vigilant and alert like a warrior bride, armored up and standing guard to protect an encampment of troops while they rest for the night.[1]

---

1. Judges 5, 6.

> **Study Prayer:**
>
> O Lord and Savior, teach your servants according to your love and teach us your decrees.
>
> A prayer according to Psalm 119:124

We go back in time to visit the tribes of Israel who couldn't wait for Moses to come down from the mountain. They gave up on him and demanded something, anything that would sate their empty spiritual yearnings. Like them, we're not very good at waiting. Because of this, the Bible is full of instruction about making good use of time, rather than wasting it. The bride of Christ waits patiently for the Bridegroom to return for her.

Daniel's life story helps us to endure with patience. He spent a night surrounded by ravenous beasts, waiting for the king to remove the stone over the lion's den in the morning. Abraham's story benefits us. He waited a quarter century before Sarah gave birth to the promised son, Isaac. We can learn from the hundred and twenty disciples who waited together several days, praying in agreement before the day of Pentecost.

The word for "wait" in Hebrew is קָוָה qâvâh.[2] It's a beautiful and meaningful word with connotations of lingering and enduring. We can visualize this Hebrew word as fibers woven into one rope made durable by braiding three strands together into one strong cord.[3] In reality, when we wait on the Lord, we're like a frail thread woven into an unbreakable three-stranded cord; the Father, Son, and Holy Spirit. There is no need for any other.

> *When the people saw that Moses was so long in coming down from the mountain, they gathered around Aaron and said, "Come, make us gods who will go before us. As for this fellow Moses who brought us up out of Egypt, we don't know what has happened to him."*
>
> (Exodus 32:1)

Jesus' followers are like a bride in waiting. But what do we do while waiting for Christ to come back for us? Will He find us serving tables? Will the poor and needy be our cause until the day He returns? Jesus modeled a life of humble service as He washed the disciples' feet. He served them bread and the cup as they reclined around the table at the Last Supper.

---

2. Psalm 27:14.
3. Ecclesiastes 4:12.

Now, as a bride in waiting, we are ambassadors of Jesus Christ and we stand with Him in the trials of the Church. We endure persecution for the sake of the cross. As pillars of the Church we are strengthened to stand firm in the faith even as the earth shakes under our feet. We are bound together as one in Christ, strengthened to wait for that great wedding banquet where we will see Him in all His glory.

As we wait, it's as if every prayer, well-spoken word, and act of love serve as fibers to strengthen the fabric for the robe the bride wears to the wedding supper of the Lamb.[4]

> *For who is greater, the one who is at the table or the one who serves? Is it not the one who is at the table? But I am among you as one who serves.*

(Luke 22:27)

When violent storms blow our way, we take refuge. News of wildfires blazing toward our home compels us to find a safe place to shelter. Tropical storm warnings propel us to find a safe harbor. In times of trouble people need a Rock in whom they can anchor their lives. Every child needs a solid foundation to build their lives on and give them a sense of security. Our heavenly Father provides the safe haven we need as we navigate the troubled waters of life.

Entering the gates into God's mighty fortress provides us with a safe place to rest. Under His covering we can pour out our hearts, casting all our anxious thoughts on Him, confident that He cares for us in every way.[5] We wait, ready, willing, and dressed in armor of light, with our feet firmly planted on the Rock, Christ Jesus, and we will not be shaken.

> *Yes, my soul, find rest in God; my hope comes from him. Truly he is my rock and my salvation; he is my fortress, I will not be shaken. My salvation and my honor depend on God; he is my mighty rock, my refuge. Trust in him at all times, you people; pour out your hearts to him, for God is our refuge.*

(Psalm 62:5–8)

When we enter a warehouse grocery store, the first several aisles in the food section are packed full of snacks with sugar as the key ingredient. It's good marketing because all people everywhere have a sweet tooth to satisfy. We fill our car up with gas and then buy a candy bar to sate our appetite until lunch.

All God's children ought to have the same kind of yearning for sweet wisdom that comes from above. We should all seek to satisfy our "wisdom tooth."

---
4. Revelation 19:8.
5. 1 Peter 5:7.

What if church foyers had shelves stocked with packages of wisdom sweets for everyone who entered? Wisdom is better than frosting on a cake. It's like honey from the Rock that satisfies us and gives us direction as we press on through life's challenges.[6] Wisdom sweetened words offer instruction for peace, comfort, and strength to all those who will hear. We should all show up at church with a shopping cart to fill with godly wisdom.

> *Know also that wisdom is like honey for you: If you find it, there is a future hope for you, and your hope will not be cut off.*

(Proverbs 24:14)

You know a child is excited about school when you find them dressed and ready before you pour your first cup of coffee. The joy of learning something new excites them and they run to the bus stop early with lunch and snacks in their backpack.

Christians ought to have this kind of excitement about fulfilling their calling in Christ. We're called to be ready to share the reason for our faith to anyone who asks. It's like getting ourselves dressed and ready, eager to answer when we get questioned about the reason for our faith. The Apostle Paul wrote to the Philippian Church encouraging them to be clothed with Christ. Now, like the Philippians, we can be dressed in garments of praise and boldly proclaim God's saving grace at every opportunity, even until our dying breath.

> *I eagerly expect and hope that I will in no way be ashamed, but will have sufficient courage so that now as always Christ will be exalted in my body, whether by life or by death.*

(Philippians 1:20)

Before the days of cell phones and text messaging it was a challenge to know when company might show up. The cook always made a little extra tuna casserole just in case the doorbell rang as the family sat down to dinner. Back in the day, a good host always prepared extra. Welcoming friends was as easy as two folding chairs and a couple more plates on the table.

We have a promise that's better than tuna casserole. The Bridegroom will return for us at a time we least expect.[7] This is a good plan. If we knew the time of His return, or the hour we would take our last breath, we could simply live as we wish and then make amends at the last minute. A better way is to live a life full of joyful expectation of our Savior's return. The best life is one that's lived in the fullness of Christ, shining out as the light of the world.

---

6. Psalm 81:16.
7. Mark 13:35–38.

When we are faithful, living in keeping with repentance, walking according to our baptism, and being clothed in God's righteousness, we are made ready. We are prepared as a bride for His coming.

> *So you also must be ready, because the Son of Man will come at an hour when you do not expect him.*
>
> (Matthew 24:44)

When a soldier stands on guard duty in the early hours of the morning, just a blink of sleep could lead to disaster. He must be constantly alert to detect camouflaged insurgents lurking in the shadows, creeping slowly toward the troop's encampment. In the dark of night, even a second of slumber causes the guard to miss a rustle in the grass or the snap of a twig.

As warriors of the cross, we are called to be constantly alert because our Redeemer promised to return unannounced, like a thief who comes in the night. We are called to be sober, awake, and eager. As we wait on alert, His righteousness shields us like a flak vest and the hope of salvation is our helmet.[8] Heaven's children belong to the day and stand guard in the night. We work in the daylight and keep watch as light fades to darkness.[9]

> *So then, let us not be like others, who are asleep, but let us be awake and sober.*
>
> (1 Thessalonians 5:6)

Fragrances of perfume and bath oils emanate from the bride's chamber as she prepares for her wedding. She is clothed with an exquisitely embroidered fine linen dress and her feet with the best leather sandals. Carefully selected jewelry made with priceless stones grace her neck in the brilliant finery of a heavenly kingdom. Precious gold and silver adorn her wrists and arms and chime with expectation. She's as beautiful as a queen in waiting, and all who hear about the luxurious adornments provided for her exclaim her splendor.[10]

She is ready and waiting with her lamp shining bright as she listens to hear the shout, "Look, the bridegroom is coming! Come out and meet him!"[11] All Christians together are the bride of Christ and called to prepare for Jesus to return as our Bridegroom. We're a bride adorned with His splendor, giving us cause to sing out with rejoicing, shout out with praise, and lift up our hands to glorify His holy name.

---

8. 1 Thessalonians 5:4–8.
9. Nehemiah 4:22.
10. Ezekiel 16:9–14.
11. Matthew 25:6 NLT.

Let us rejoice and be glad and give him glory! For the wedding of the Lamb has come, and his bride has made herself ready.

(Revelation 19:7)

The bridesmaids stand ready, holding up the fine linen robe for the bride to wear at the wedding banquet. The room is abuzz with expectation as her attendants flutter about with preparations. The bride gets ready so she can wait, prepared for the Bridegroom who is promised to her.

Most of us are not very good at waiting. We're texting or reading news updates on our cell phones to keep our minds off the long line ahead of us. The Bible has numerous accounts of those who failed at waiting, and others who were strengthened in waiting. Their failures and successes help us learn and overcome our impatient habits. It's good to know that waiting is not an inactive, recliner chair kind of thing. It's more like keeping our hands busy braiding a rope with many strands to make it strong. It's like weaving a fine fabric for a beautiful wedding garment.

When we have to wait, like at the grocery checkout stand, our sweet craving calls for a bit of chocolate candy to satisfy it, and it's right there to tempt us. Wouldn't it be better to cultivate our "wisdom tooth" by satisfying it with God's words of wisdom? For all those who are in Christ, wisdom is sweetness for our soul and fully satisfies with its many benefits.

The Church is a bride who waits, pledged in covenant. We are called to be ready to give an answer for the hope we have in Christ. Can we live with joyful expectation in the tangles of life's jungle? How is it possible to face all the chaos in the world around us with a sense of peace and rest? We have the answer inscribed on our hearts and, because of this, we're always ready to present Christ who is our eternal hope. We prevail like a soldier who stands ready, armored with faith and hope and salvation for a helmet. At the same time, the Church is like a bride delightfully adorned as beautiful as a queen; a bride dressed and ready for our Bridegroom's promised return.

Chapter 10

Dressed and Ready

Q & A

1. Why is it so hard to wait patiently for what is promised to us?
___
___
___

2. What can we do while waiting for our Bridegroom to return?
___
___
___

3. How do we satisfy our "wisdom tooth," and why is it so important?
___
___
___

4. How does a bride store up oil for her lamp?
___
___
___

My Journal Notes:

A Joyful Bride

Key Scripture:

- "I will betroth you to me forever; I will betroth you in righteousness and justice, in love and compassion. I will betroth you in faithfulness, and you will acknowledge the Lord." (Hosea 2:19–20)

This lesson opens our hearts to the abundant joys that belong to all who wait with eager expectation for Christ's return. We'll come to know more of our Bridegroom's eternal love and faithful affection. And we, in turn, joyfully proclaim Him as our very own. As diligent students, we dig deeper into the Scriptures to explore the mystery of Christ who indwells us. The Word and the Spirit show us that His holy presence is complete when we also abide in Him. As we prayerfully open our Bibles, the pieces of this great puzzle come together.

> Study Prayer:
>
> *O Lord our Redeemer, teach us knowledge and good judgment, for we trust your commands.*
>
> A prayer from Psalm 119:66

All Christians are espoused to Creator God who husbands us.[1] Christ Jesus is gathering together a Church to be His bride. He serves as High Priest of this union and ministers grace, mercy, forgiveness, love, and so much more than we can imagine. He pours out His affections on His people, the Church.[2] He heals, restores, and cleanses us in body, soul, and spirit. We rejoice in His name: Yahweh, Lord of Hosts. And He gives us a new name; His name to mark us as His own.

We are wrapped with a sense of comfort and security. Our confidence in God's enduring love heartens us. His name, given to us as our new name,

---

1. Isaiah 54:5.
2. Philippians 1:8.

covers us with a shield. With His name as our covering, we can be confident in His protection and comfort. When an enemy attacks with their fiery arrows, we stand secure at His side, bold and confident. We know our Father is mighty in battle—the Lord of Hosts is His name.

> *For your Maker is your husband–the Lord Almighty is his name–the Holy One of Israel is your Redeemer; he is called the God of all the earth.*

(Isaiah 54:5)

As a husband and wife are wedded together, we have cause for joyful celebration. The guests dress up in their finest clothes, apply their best cologne, and practice their dance steps. What do we enjoy most at wedding receptions? Feasting and dancing! Why do we feast and dance? Because we're so happy to see love create a new family. Those who are in Christ prepare themselves for the Bridegroom's great wedding feast. We can practice our dance steps while our feet are still set here on terra firma. Hope springs eternal to fill us with joy and peace as we wait to hear the great wedding supper announced with a shout. We rejoice because of our abundant expectation, watching and listening to hear the call for our Bridegroom's arrival.

As this day of celebration comes closer there is rejoicing in heaven and earth.[3] Jesus is preparing a place for us, just like the groom who prepares a home where he will carry his bride over the threshold.[4] Listen to hear the great assembly sing the Bridegroom's new song.[5] Join with the congregation and shout out with joyful anticipation. The bride-in-waiting sings out from the depths of her heart and soul in harmony with Christ who leads the Church in joyful chorus.

> *As a young man marries a young woman, so will your Builder marry you; as a bridegroom rejoices over his bride, so will your God rejoice over you.*

(Isaiah 62:5)

Weddings are a once in a lifetime event for a couple. We enrich the ceremony with a flower petal pathway for the bride to walk down the aisle. Family and friends stand and watch her as she holds her dad's arm and skips her way to the altar. Celebrative dances with the bride, toasts, gifts, and congratulations follow a ceremony that joins the bride and groom together as a new family.

Jesus taught the crowds and His disciples with many parables, revealing His kingdom by drawing word pictures the hearer could relate to and un-

---
3. Psalm 96:11.
4. John 14:3.
5. Psalm 149:1.

derstand. He taught about the kingdom of God with stories that reveal the mysteries of the kingdom. He taught in parables to present the Church as His bride in waiting. His stories make it clear that "many are invited, but few are chosen."[6] Those who are invited and accept the invitation can look forward to the wedding feast with an attitude of joyful celebration. This jubilant mindset overflows from those who Christ indwells and who abide in Him.

> *The kingdom of heaven is like a king who prepared a wedding banquet for his son.*

(Matthew 22:2)

Running a three-legged race teaches kids the challenges of working in step with each other. If a pair of runners can't agree on how they'll work together to reach the goal line, they fall on their faces. To win the race, they need to coordinate their legs and head straight for the goal line. In the same way a new bride and groom have to learn to live in agreement.

But it's a challenge for fallible people to work together. Our individuality works against us. We need to overcome this default mode. We see Christ Jesus as our High Priest who ministers to us, but then our attitude turns to thoughts like, "Okay, Jesus. What have you done for me lately?" We're like people who enjoy watching someone else dance but refuse to dance with them.[7]

It's hard for a bride and groom to do everything in harmony. But two people can't walk together unless they agree on their destination.[8] This kind of agreement doesn't come easy. But we are a unique people, called and chosen to be united in Christ so that we may run the race as one with Christ and His Church.

> *"Return, faithless people," declares the Lord, "for I am your husband. I will choose you—one from a town and two from a clan—and bring you to Zion."*

(Jeremiah 3:14)

Most weddings require months of preparation. Endless details need special attention, reservations, appointments, and fittings. Imagine planning a wedding when you don't know the time or day the groom will come. When the invitations are sent out, instead of a date, time, and location, it says, "Be dressed and ready when he comes." The men shave, slap on some cologne, brush the dust off their dancing shoes, and throw on their best shirt and pants. The ladies spend time in front of their mirrors, and then put on their jewelry and wedding dresses. Now they're all ready, but when is the groom coming? They don't know.

---
6. Matthew 22:14.
7. Matthew 11:17.
8. Amos 3:3.

So, what do we do? Do we put our pajamas back on and binge watch a new TV series? No, we get to work, continually preparing ourselves. We search the Scriptures to grow in grace and knowledge of our Lord and Savior Jesus Christ. By the power of the Word and the Holy Spirit we store up the oil we need for the long night's watch. We bind ourselves to the Lord as we wait with expectation to hear the trumpets sound to announce His coming. All those who are in Christ shine out with His light so that others may be enlightened by it.

> *But while they were on their way to buy the oil, the bridegroom arrived. The virgins who were ready went in with him to the wedding banquet. And the door was shut.*
>
> (Matthew 25:10)

The word of the Lord raised up troops from a valley of dry bones.[9] Then the thundering footfalls of a mighty army shook the ground as they marched forward. God's servant prophesied as instructed and sun-bleached bones were covered with flesh. He prophesied again and the Spirit breathed the four winds into those who were slain. Then they rose up as if birthed from the womb at the first light of dawn.[10]

They rose up and covered themselves in the splendor of the Lord's armor of light, a mighty army, ready and willing for the Almighty to lead them forward into battle. This army doesn't know the day or hour they will be called to march out, but they give a mighty shout with confidence because they are trained, fully prepared every moment of the day and night.

Revive us, O Lord so that we stand ready in Christ who has redeemed us.

> *Your troops will be willing on your day of battle. Arrayed in holy splendor, your young men will come to you like dew from the morning's womb.*
>
> (Psalm 110:3)

On bended knee, a young man asks, "Will you be my bride?"

The answer to his question is a joyful "yes," followed by embraces and tears of joy. This moment of bliss begins months of careful preparation. She selects the perfect wedding dress with its train and veil. The bride prepares her trousseau with jubilant expectation. The guest list is finalized and the wedding invitations are sent out. This is a time of active and joyful preparation.

The Church is the betrothed bride of Christ. We prepare ourselves as a bride by working together for the great wedding banquet. We confess our

---

9. Ezekiel 37:1–13.
10. Psalm 110:3.

faults to each other.[11] We build up and strengthen our brothers and sisters who gather to worship with us. As we grow in grace and knowledge we learn to walk together in agreement, shoulder to shoulder in the work of the Great Commission. As one in Christ we lift up and encourage all those in our community of faith. Each one of us is called to serve according to the anointing and gifting work of the Holy Spirit as we prepare ourselves for the Bridegroom's return.

We don't know the day or the hour of His return, so we must be dressed and ready at all times. Diligence, perseverance, faithfulness, and love are watchwords to guide our steps every day. We put on the armor of light and rise up like a mighty army, troops raised to life so they may be ready and willing, abiding in Christ until the day of the Lord.

The great wedding day is near and it takes a lifetime to prepare ourselves. Our days in waiting are filled with the work of our calling. So, let's stand up, take up our cross, and let the Light of the World who indwells us shine out for the honor and glory of our promised Bridegroom.

---

11. James 5:16.

Chapter 11

A Joyful Bride

Q & A

1. Why are believers given a new name when they come to saving faith in Jesus Christ?

2. Why is it so difficult for people to work together in harmony?

3. How is it possible to be dressed and ready for the Bridegroom when we don't know the day or time of His return?

My Journal Notes:

March Forward in the Light

Key Scriptures:

- "By this we may be sure that we are in him: whoever says, 'I abide in him,' ought to walk just as he walked." (1 John 2:5–6)
- "For in him the whole fullness of deity dwells bodily, and you have come to fullness in him, who is the head of every ruler and authority. In him also you were circumcised with a spiritual circumcision, by putting off the body of the flesh in the circumcision of Christ; when you were buried with him in baptism, you were also raised with him through faith in the power of God, who raised him from the dead." (Colossians 2:9–12)

This study portrays a covenant relationship with our Lord and Savior as a two way bond. Our covenant is sealed with a Redeemer's promise, giving us confidence and a sense of security, knowing that Christ indwells us. At church summer camp kids are taught that Jesus wants to live in their hearts. Then, as they mature in their faith, they come to know the Spirit of Christ who desires to inhabit His people. It's easy to forget our part in the plan. We are, in turn, called to abide in Christ. As He indwells us we are beckoned to dwell in Him, and then urged to remain in Him. The Scriptures in this study remind us that our relationship with the Father, Son, and Holy Spirit is complete as we are bound together with the Triune God. This is the reason our Savior admonishes us to "remain in me."[1]

Our full-circle relationship is torn down by complacent attitudes. When people say, "I've got Jesus in my heart and that's all I need," it's as if self-satisfied Christians have a spiritual light dimmer switch or a volume control that adjusts their relationship with Christ according to what they need or want in the moment.

When the Holy Spirit convicts of sin, a contrite heart turns up the volume. A pretentious heart changes the channel. It's only after they get them-

---
1. John 15:4.

selves in trouble that they turn on the light to find a way out of their mess. Test yourself to see if this is true for you. Do you wait to tune in and listen to what the Bible says about lifting your burdens only after the burden gets too heavy? Too often we treat Jesus as if He's our 911 call. Our heavenly Father promises to be an ever-present help in times of trouble, but heaven's emergency dispatch system doesn't always work the way we like.[2]

This lesson prepares us to march forward with Christ as our banner. We'll learn that we cannot be ready if our Christian life is little more than a crisis hotline. In Christ we are brought into a covenant relationship. This means that the Spirit of Christ indwells us. It also means that we are made one with Christ in His suffering, death, burial, and resurrection. By the power of the cross we enter into the fullness of Christ and His strength. By faith we enter into the kingdom of heaven where He is head over every power and authority. In Christ, by the authority of the Word and the work of the Spirit, we are set free from the power of the flesh. It's cut away so that we are no longer subject to the pull of our mortal longings. We are strengthened in our soul and spirit to overcome what the Bible calls "desires of the flesh."[3]

Let's press on to learn more of our covenant relationship that calls us to walk, to speak, and to reach out our hands just as Jesus did when He came to earth as Immanuel, God with us. That's impossible, right? Marching out ready for battle is unachievable in our own strength or by our own means.[4] An empowered Christ-like life is only possible by the anointing work of the Holy Spirit who indwells us. He makes us new creations so that we may abide in Christ and rise up fully armored.

> Study Prayer:
>
> *Help us to continue in the teaching of Christ so we may have both the Father and the Son.*
>
> A prayer according to 2 John 2:9

Our Lord and Savior is likened to a vine that flourishes in the realm of God's kingdom. We were once like wild shoots that are now grafted into the Vine, who is Jesus the Christ. As a grafted branch we grow together with the vine, draw our nutrients from the vine, and produce its fruit. Unlike branches permanently grafted into good rootstock in our garden, we need to be encouraged to remain in Christ and bear the fruit of the Spirit of Christ.

---

2. Proverbs 1:24–33.
3. Galatians 5:15-16.
4. Zechariah 4:6.

This is a full-circle covenantal relationship. The vine provides nutrients, and then we produce the fruit of the vine; all for God's glory and honor. For us to be fruitful, we must simply remain grafted into Christ. All those who are called by God's holy name are grafted into the Vine, who is Christ Jesus. This is a safe place to grow and flourish even when weeds and brambles try to choke us out. As branches of the Vine, we receive sustenance that makes us produce good fruit. But we have the ability to control the flow of this life-giving nourishment. We have a choice. Will we turn God's word on high volume as we stand in His counsel or turn it down low and get just enough nutrients to help us survive?

> *Remain in me, as I also remain in you. No branch can bear fruit by itself; it must remain in the vine. Neither can you bear fruit unless you remain in me.*

(John 15:4)

It's with great joy that we first hear, believe, and receive the promises of the Gospel. When the Good Shepherd brings a lost soul home, this is cause for heaven's angels to rejoice and celebrate with us. Salvation's light shines brighter than stadium flood lights turned on in the dark of the night. The volume of heaven's music gets turned up so we can joyfully dance with the saints who have gone before us. As new creations in Christ we have every reason to overflow with joy.

But the trials of life and the cruel realities of the world get us down. The Tempter tries to trip us up and drag us back into the darkness of sin and depravity. It's as if weeds try to choke out the best seeds planted in our garden. All too soon we're confronted with a major life decision: will we go back to walking on a broad and easy highway or march on with Jesus in the light of His narrow path?

As true sons and daughters of the Most High God we are called to persevere. We're encouraged to press on in the faith and overcome the obstacles. Our faith in Jesus Christ compels us to live like Him and to live obedient in Him. Love for Christ draws us into sweet fellowship in Him and His body the Church. We gather together so that we may grow in grace and knowledge; taught by those who are anointed to teach. In all this we step forward in our faith, living a life that overflows with thanksgiving and praise.

> *So then, just as you received Christ Jesus as Lord, continue to live your lives in him, rooted and built up in him, strengthened in the faith as you were taught, and overflowing with thankfulness.*

(Colossians 2:6–7)

In Christ we have a sure promise that He will never leave us nor forsake us. When we hear this rock-solid promise, we can stand on it knowing He is always present with us and He is coming back for us. But we have that volume control at our disposal. Standing in God's council while on low volume means our ears will not hear. When our hearing is turned too low our faith in His promises is diminished. This lack of hearing affects our knowledge and confidence.

When we turn our spiritual amplifiers to the lowest volume all our senses grow faint. We can't step forward with confidence without the full richness of God's Word to light life's pathway. We become like people who stumble along an unfamiliar path in the dark. We need an eternal confidence that can only come by hearing with clarity and then following the precepts of Scripture.[5] The Bible's insights prepare us as a warrior bride, armored and ready for the return of our victorious Lord and Savior.

> *And now, dear children, continue in him, so that when he appears we may be confident and unashamed before him at his coming.*

(1 John 2:28)

Getting buried is a rather permanent thing. But it's much different for those who come to saving faith. We die to self, and then offer ourselves to our Savior as living sacrifices.[6] The challenge is that all too often live sacrifices get restless and go back to what is familiar and comfortable. Dying with Christ in holy baptism is to be raised up to live in the power of the resurrected Savior.

The Apostle Paul knew about human weaknesses and admonished us to continue on in the faith and live in the power of the resurrected Christ. His inspired epistles encourage us to hold fast to our faith and remain in Christ. Living in the power of His resurrection strengthens us so we may enter into the fullness of God's kingdom. Those who abide in Christ and seek His righteousness for His name's sake have no fear of falling from their secure position in Christ.[7]

> *We were therefore buried with him through baptism into death in order that, just as Christ was raised from the dead through the glory of the Father, we too may live a new life.*

(Romans 6:4)

There's an old story about a Native American who regularly won the Omak Stampede's Suicide Race. He raced his blind horse down a 225 foot

---

5. Hebrews 4:16.
6. Romans 12:1.
7. 2 Peter 3:17.

bluff to the river where they waded or swam across and then dashed to victory at the finish line in the arena. His winning streak is credited to the horse's total trust in his rider.[8]

A walk of faith is not blind, but abounds with trust. Hearing a Bible verse is like a gentle nudge that can redirect our whole day. The gentle tug of the Holy Spirit can change our direction. The encouragement of a godly friend helps us know the right way. It's always better when we walk according to what we believe and not according to personal experience. Our faith is not based on what we see. Instead, it's a child-like trust. Seeing the world's troubles and all the resulting chaos only distracts us from gaining victory over life's obstacles.

For we live by faith, not by sight.

(2 Corinthians 5:7)

When a family piles into the minivan to go to church, it's like embarking on a pilgrimage. With the kiddos buckled in their seats and sippy cups handy, we head off with a clear purpose. Then the family gathers to worship and receive the ministries of Jesus Christ our High Priest. The whole family enters into fellowship with our Savior and with other Christians. The Word teaches us so we may learn and grow in grace and knowledge of our Lord and Savior. In turn, we teach our children and disciple fellow pilgrims who seek to know the Lord.

In our gatherings we hear what our Father intends for our family and then we agree together in earnest prayers and petitions according to His desires. In our worship assemblies we are armored up with the whole armor of God that shields us from the fiery arrows of the enemy. Together we lift up our leaders and our nation so that we may live in peace.[9] As one in Christ we come to the Lord's Table as participants in and partakers of our Lord and Savior. We drink from the cup and eat the bread of communion. At this table pilgrims are strengthened to march out and serve as salt and light in our communities and our workplaces.

All of what we do in communal worship is centered in Christ, focused on exalting the Father, and empowered in the Holy Spirit. Our worship and praise must not be egocentric, but Christocentric, Theocentric, and in accord with the Spirit and all truth.[10] This clear focus keeps us from slipping into a soulish kind of worship that only meets our personal preferences and leaves the Spirit of Christ on the shelf until there's an emergency.

---

8. A local oral tradition in Omak, Washington.
9. 1 Timothy 2:1–4.
10. Galatians 5:16.

Christocentric worship is spiritual and real. We sing reverent exaltations in accord with Spirit and all truth. Our songs flow out from joyful spirits and focus on the Almighty as He has revealed Himself. True and genuine worship exalts the Spirit who breathes life into us. A congregation that worships as one in Jesus' name pushes aside all self-centered desires and then sings out with praises in the light of the bright Morning Star.[11] Our worshipful gatherings lift up Christ who indwells us so God's pilgrims can be light in a world of chaos.

> *Yet a time is coming and has now come when the true worshipers will worship the Father in the Spirit and in truth, for they are the kind of worshipers the Father seeks. God is spirit, and his worshipers must worship in the Spirit and in truth.*

(John 4:23–24)

Whether we're in prison, like the Apostle Paul, or freely going about our everyday lives, we have a calling to fulfill. Digging in to do a job the Holy Spirit assigns to us is an important part of living in covenant with Christ. When we do kingdom work, it's equally important to live our daily life in a way that honors our life's mission and the name of Christ our Savior. If we carry out kingdom tasks but then live like hell, the good things we have done will be forgotten.[12] Even worse, our good works will be stained by our sin until the day we repent and turn back to Christ for forgiveness and cleansing.

Everyone who is called by the Father's holy name is given a good work to complete. It's an impossible task that is made possible by the Spirit of Christ at work in us and through us. Indeed, God is faithful to complete every good work that He ordained.[13] When the battle is won, our work is done and God calls us home, there is a great reward for us who live and serve faithfully in the light of Christ.

> *As a prisoner for the Lord, then, I urge you to live a life worthy of the calling you have received.*

(Ephesians 4:1)

Daniel and three of his fellow exiles offer a great example of the effect of living in accord with God's holy presence. The nation of Israel was overthrown because of their sin and God's people were exiled to Babylon. The articles of worship in Jerusalem's temple were plundered and placed in the house of Nebuchadnezzar's god. These four men and many others were pressed into service of Babylon's king. While in preparation for their work in this foreign land, they were offered a royal diet and given foreign names.

---

11. See Chapter 1 in author's book: Great Separations.
12. Ezekiel 18:24.
13. Philippians 1:6.

But Daniel, Hananiah, Mishael, and Azariah determined to remain true and acted in agreement with God's holy presence. They feared the God of Israel more than the king of Babylon. As exiles in a strange land with a foreign tongue they continued to live according to the precepts of their omnipresent Father. They refused the rich foods and drink from the king's table and ate a simple diet of vegetables and water instead. They kept on dwelling in Yahweh's presence. Even in a foreign land, their heart's continued to reside in a kingdom where knowledge, wisdom, insight, and understanding were poured out with abundance.

But Daniel resolved not to defile himself with the royal food and wine, and he asked the chief official for permission not to defile himself this way.

(Daniel 1:8)

In every matter of wisdom and understanding about which the king questioned them, he found them ten times better than all the magicians and enchanters in his whole kingdom.

(Daniel 1:20)

Our faith journey is more than a hand-in-hand kind of walk. It's a joining of our hearts—an all-embracing relationship with our Savior. All God's children were once like unproductive wild shoots, but we are brought into covenant and grafted into the Vine. This is a joyful relationship, but we must resist the appeals of self-serving pacifiers that drag us back into the dregs of darkness. We must march on in our faith and live in keeping with our baptism that makes us one with Christ Jesus. This truth is vital because living outside our covenant disconnects us from Christ victorious, who is the Head of the Church.

It's not a good plan to walk according to what we see or feel. The world's messages are like bright, flashing neon lights to tempt us and draw us back to our old way of living. But it's better to press on, keeping our eyes fixed on the mark for the prize of our high calling.[14] We can walk by faith, not distracted by fearsome things we see pressing in on us.

Our covenant is relational. The love of Christ compels us to take a pilgrimage to gather and worship. In our worship assemblies we receive the ministries of our High Priest, Jesus Christ. Then in turn we lift up holy hands and shout out with praises to exalt and glorify our God and Father. In our assemblies we are armored up, strengthened, and anointed so that we may do the work ordained for each of us to do. We are empowered by the Holy Spirit to go out and speak what Jesus is speaking, touch whom He is touching,

---

14. Philippians 3:14.

and go where He is going. All those who are faithful in their calling can look forward to the awesome reward waiting for them in glory.

You ought to live holy and godly lives as you look forward to the day of God and speed its coming.

(2 Peter 3:11–12)

The Bible likens us to sheep. James, in his epistle, says we're like horses that need bits in their mouths to make them obey. We also need blinders to keep us from being drawn in by the world's distractions. To keep us close to the heart of Yahweh, our God, we need to take regular pilgrimages, gathering with people of faith where we are strengthened together so that we may press forward in this chaotic world. In our assemblies we worship, serve, and minister according to our calling and in keeping with our covenant of love. Then we march out into the world to be the light of Christ, doing acts of true kindness and love-inspired deeds of a true servant.

We must turn our Bible's volume on full blast to strengthen us. This makes it possible to be in the world and not succumb to its darkness as it tries to press in on us. When we focus our lives on the Scriptures, we grow stronger to resist the attractions of the world's flashing neon lights. Living in the Word and continuing to walk in Christ keeps us safe in the kingdom of light where there is an abundance of godly wisdom, knowledge, and understanding. This is many times better than all earthbound wisdom. These abundant blessings are great benefits for those who march on in the light of faith, abide in Christ, and live in keeping with His holy presence.

Chapter 12

March Forward in the Light

Q & A

1. Is it possible for fallible people to live a Christ-like life in a fallen world?

2. Describe a covenantal relationship with the Father, Son, and Holy Spirit.

3. Why is it so important for us to gather together with other Christians to minister, serve, and worship before Jesus our High Priest?

4. Does it really matter if our Christian work and ministry is inconsistent with the lives we live every day?

My Journal Notes:

Overcomers in Christ

Key Scripture:

- "Anyone who runs ahead and does not continue in the teaching of Christ does not have God; whoever continues in the teaching has both the Father and the Son." (2 John 9)

Americans have great admiration for rugged individuality. We look up to mavericks who ride alone across rugged desert terrain into the foothills where the sun sets. We have a "pull yourself up by your own bootstraps" mentality. But another popular phrase, "No man is an island," brings us closer to reality. This study leads us to a greater understanding of waiting on the Lord that is both active and productive. We'll learn that waiting is a joint venture where we must work in unison.

> Study Prayer:
>
> *O Lord our ever-present help,*
> *may our eyes be blessed to see and our ears blessed to hear.*
>
> A prayer according to Matthew 13:16.

In the realm of the kingdom of heaven, no one is self-sufficient. Every working part of the body of Christ must rely on strength, comfort, and unity in Christ with other parts in order to survive and thrive. Those who are called to do the work of the kingdom of heaven become one working part of the whole. This interactive system is more than just talk. We can't claim to be a gear in the works when we're laying in the bottom of the oil pan among the metal shavings.

When we watch an expert auto technician at work, we learn that one important part of their job is to patiently inspect and clean the parts before reassembling them. Every engine part gets examined under a magnifying lamp to be sure it will work as designed. Then it is bathed in acid before it's installed.

Now let's apply our shop talk to the kingdom of heaven. We're a lot like small gears in a big engine. Sooner or later we all fail. But when we admit our failure, we're ready for repair. When we're examined in the light of God's word, we must repent. Then we're forgiven, washed in the blood of the Lamb, and restored to serving as a useful part in the body of Christ. Hopefully, we're good for another hundred thousand miles of working in unison with all the other parts.

> *If we claim to have fellowship with him and yet walk in the darkness, we lie and do not live out the truth. But if we walk in the light, as he is in the light, we have fellowship with one another, and the blood of Jesus, his Son, purifies us from all sin.*

(1 John 1:6–7)

A dad is all talk and no show if he showers his kids with promises of love, favors, and gifts, but never attends their soccer games like he said he would. When he agrees to come watch his daughter act as Mother Mary in the Christmas pageant, but doesn't show up, he's like a thief who steals dreams. He's not a real dad. He talks like a dad, and he likes to think of himself as a good dad, but if he truthfully examined himself the facts would prove otherwise.

The Apostle Paul teaches us to take an account ourselves to see if we remain in the faith.[1] Are we all talk and no show? Do we make big promises and then let them go as if words mean nothing? We're fallible people and we need to check up on ourselves, using the Scriptures as our standard of measure. Waiting on the Lord helps to guide us as we take a regular spiritual inventory of ourselves. With our inventory complete, we have an opportunity to repent, be forgiven, change course, and then come before our heavenly Father with confidence, knowing that we are faithful and obedient in Christ.

> *Dear children, let's not merely say that we love each other; let us show the truth by our actions. Our actions will show that we belong to the truth, so we will be confident when we stand before God.*

(1 John 3:18–19 NLT)

Fulfilling the command of the Gospel is clear and simple: believe in the name of God's Son, Jesus Christ, and love one another as He commanded us.[2] The Good News message is plain and straightforward: believe and be baptized.[3] Can we say, "I believe in Christ as my Savior, so just leave me

---

1. 2 Corinthians 13:5.
2. 1 John 3:23.
3. Mark 16:16.

alone?" If this is all we do, we're like a seed that germinates, breaks through the soil, and then gets choked out by the cares of this world before it can produce fruit.[4]

It's important to understand that saving faith brings us into a covenant relationship. The love planted in our hearts is more than a quick sprout in shallow soil. It is a call to act in agreement with Christ's holy indwelling presence. Trusting in Christ compels us to act according to the seed of faith planted in us. Will the seed of our faith simply shoot up and wither, or will it grow, flourish, and produce good fruit for the kingdom of heaven?

A sprouting faith needs to be watered from the Spring of Living Water. Struggling seedlings need nourishment from the holy Scriptures. New growth needs the Light of the World to make it flourish. Unlike garden seeds that naturally produce according to their created genetic code, God's children have to make wise choices every moment of their day. Will we choose to obey the Almighty's commands, or will we cut ourselves off from the Light of Life, the nourishment of the Word, and the Springs of Living Water? Producing good fruit isn't difficult. It's a matter of putting self aside and waiting on the Lord, resting in the Lord, and remaining in Christ, who is the true Vine. Abundant fruitfulness is quite easy for those who wait.[5]

> *This is how we know that we love the children of God: by loving God and carrying out his commands. In fact, this is love for God: to keep his commands. And his commands are not burdensome.*

(1 John 5:2–3)

People who trip up are quick to protest: "What do you expect? I'm not perfect!" In reality, we're all much worse than "not perfect." We're fatally flawed. Even those who want to do what is right before God are constantly confronted with their imperfections.[6] We're new creations in Christ with an old selfish nature that constantly battles to regain its power over us. Yes, in Christ we have died to sin. It has lost its power over us, but the "before Christ" part of us uses a lot of tricky battle tactics in its attempt to make a comeback. For this reason, we're called to overcome this mortal nature and press on. Victory is only possible in Christ's holy presence.

Consider what all Christians are faced with. We're held to a standard of perfection that's impossible for any mortal. We're called to live a sinless life just as Jesus walked, but we constantly slip up. We're told to be strong, but we have no strength of our own. We're commanded to be bold, but panic makes

---

4. Mark 4:19.
5. Isaiah 40:31.
6. Matthew 5:48.

our knees knock when we put on Gospel shoes. We're seriously defective people, and because of this we have a great need to remain in His holy presence forgiven and cleansed.

When we do fail and fall into sin, we have cause to rejoice; not in our sin but in the Lord who forgives us and cleanses us. We can delight in God's power that is best shown through weak, forgiven vessels. We celebrate and sing out God's praises because of the Lord's faithfulness. There is comfort in Jesus' presence because He is our advocate with the Father. We don't have to continue in sin's death grip because we are free of its chains. There is no need to wallow in "I'm not perfect" excuses.

All fear and doubt must be tossed out. We must stop focusing on our limitations and wait in the presence of the Spirit of Christ. Partakers of Christ overcome their fatal imperfections because His righteousness encompasses us to perfect us, make us Christlike, and unite us into a holy nation.

> *His divine power has given us everything we need for a godly life through our knowledge of him who called us by his own glory and goodness. Through these he has given us his very great and precious promises, so that through them you may participate in the divine nature, having escaped the corruption in the world caused by evil desires.*

(2 Peter 1:3–4)

Life on planet Earth is a long journey on roads cluttered with hazards. Our path has a lot of hairpin turns on precarious cliffside roads with few guardrails. Remember Jacob who walked this kind of path on his desert journey? After sleeping on a rock for his pillow all night, the Lord came to him in a dream to give him a promise of His presence. This promise continues to cover each one of us today.

Whether we're locked behind bars in prison or quarantined in a back bedroom, the Lord of Hosts holds us in the hollow of His hands. Neither imprisonment nor plague nor pestilence can separate us from the presence of Yahweh and His cover of protection. No diagnosis or prognosis will ever remove us from the watchful care of our Lord and Savior. Rest assured that neither abuse, violence, nor tormenting words can steal us away from our Savior's holy presence.[7]

> *I am with you and will watch over you wherever you go, and I will bring you back to this land. I will not leave you until I have done what I have promised you.*

(Genesis 28:15)

---

7. Romans 8:38–39.

Overcomers in Christ can prepare and wait with confident assurance. We look forward to a victory that is as sure as the Rock in whom we stand. We learn from Moses, another hero of our faith. He heard the Great I AM speak to reassure him that his God is faithful. This promise continues to be fulfilled in Yeshua, our Messiah even for us today.

Moses was assigned an impossible task. He spent forty years as a shepherd in the wilderness, a refugee from Egypt. Then, the Almighty called him to deliver and then lead His nation. He was called to serve as God's messenger to Pharoah, but he tried to excuse himself because of his halting speech. Moses knew his weaknesses. He knew the task was too much for any mortal man, and he asked for the Lord's Presence to go with him so the people would know they were a nation set apart from all other nations as a holy people.

Then the Lord told Moses: "I will do the very thing you have asked, because I am pleased with you and I know you by name."[8] The Creator of all heaven and earth hasn't changed. He knows our name. A bold confidence washes through us because he calls us by name. We know His presence never leaves us, He never forsakes us, and He brings us into His eternal rest.

The Lord replied, "My Presence will go with you, and I will give you rest."

(Exodus 33:14)

After blinking our eyes awake in the morning, it often feels like there are growling lions ready to confront us when we step out the front door.[9] It takes a lot more than a double espresso to drive back these fears. It's important to take time to enter into God's holy presence with thanksgiving and praise, lay our troubles before Him, and wait in the Father's counsel. In doing this we come into the presence and protection of God's armor so we can be sent out and confront the lions head on.

The stories of faith and victory in the Old Testament build our confidence so that we can stand firm in the presence of the Lord of the Armies of Heaven. As an example: Jonathan and his armor bearer defeated a whole army.[10] Later, Israel's army retreated, leaving one of David's mighty men behind enemy lines. No problem! Eleazar took his sword in hand and kept swinging until the Lord gave Israel a great victory.[11] These impossible tasks were made possible because of God's holy presence.

In Christ, we are not called to defend a holy nation. But we are given a job that no mortal person can do by themselves. Our work is just as impossi-

---
8. Exodus 33:17.
9. Proverbs 26:13.
10. 1 Samuel 14:1–23.
11. 2 Samuel 23:10.

ble as one man against an entire enemy garrison. The Lord who calls us to serve is ever-present with us to accomplish all that he desires. Indeed, He uses impossible people to accomplish impossible tasks.

> *When you go to war against your enemies and see horses and chariots and an army greater than yours, do not be afraid of them, because the Lord your God, who brought you up out of Egypt, will be with you.*

(Deuteronomy 20:1).

The Lord Almighty can certainly use one person to defeat a vast army, but we must remember that we don't stand alone in our faith. We need each other to benefit from the collective wisdom and strength of the whole community of faith. This unity is important because we make each other better people just as iron sharpens iron.[12]

A young boy named David stood alone against a hulk of a man, and he used one stone to slay that giant. Jonathan defeated a whole army single-handed. Eleazar stood alone to win a great victory for Israel; but were they really alone in their victories? We know the right answer: "Of course not." The presence of the Lord was with them. But equally important: they served as one working part within the whole realm. If they turned away from God's holy nation, separating themselves from Yahweh's holy presence, they would have been soundly defeated.

We are made part of a royal priesthood to serve in the Church. We press on to fight in the strength of the Lord. We can be sure that our Creator is present to guide us in life's loneliest battles. But His holy presence becomes even more effective as we all come together in His name. There is victory as we abide in Christ who is ever-present with us in our worship gatherings. We're armored up as we stand together in community. When we assemble together in Jesus' name, He is actively present to minister to us as our High Priest, strengthening us to go out and fight the kingdom's battles, whether alone or as a mighty army.

> *Surely you need guidance to wage war, and victory is won through many advisers.*

(Proverbs 24:6)

An old saying warns that trouble comes in threes. The prophet Isaiah may have thought about this adage when he proclaimed the Lord's safekeeping presence through three kinds of disasters.[13]

---

12. Proverbs 27:17.
13. Isaiah 43:2.

1. When we pass through turbulent waters, the Almighty says; "I will be with you."
2. When the rivers rise and rage against us and our homes, the Great I AM promises they will not sweep us away.
3. When wildfires encroach with their flames devouring everything around us, our heavenly Father promises we will not be burned.

It builds our faith to know the historic roots of the promises of the Lord's presence and protection when triple threats come against us. No doubt Isaiah wrote his inspired words because he walked in the sandals of Israel's twelve tribes as they escaped slavery in Egypt and then finally crossed the Jordan River into the Promised Land.

4. Yehovah God's cloud covered Israel, parting the waters as they passed through the Red Sea to escape the Egyptian Army.
5. The God of Abraham held back the raging flood waters of the Jordan River so the people could cross over into a Land flowing with milk and honey.
6. Israel marched around Jericho as the Lord instructed and the town was crushed and burned while the twelve tribes passed by in safety.[14]

Through all of life's battles, tests, and trials, the Lord God is more than able to deliver us out of them all and bring us home to our eternal Promised Land where we will dwell in His presence forever. We serve an awesome God.

> *When you pass through the waters, I will be with you; and when you pass through the rivers, they will not sweep over you. When you walk through the fire, you will not be burned; the flames will not set you ablaze. For I am the Lord your God, the Holy One of Israel, your Savior.*

(Isaiah 43:2–3)

At every intersection of life and at every turn in the road we are confronted with giant obstacles that are impossible for us to defeat on our own. It's terrifying to confront and we find ourselves pressed to decide: flight or fight? Will we turn and run away from this tyrant, or will we stand up fully armored in the Lord to ward off the Goliath?

It is only possible to stand against impossible odds when we wait in the presence of the Lord Almighty. Our own strength and ability offer no good reason for confidence. But when we know that Christ Jesus our Lord indwells us, and that we live in agreement with His holy indwelling presence, even the smallest stone in our pocket can slay a giant. This is the victorious kind of living that prepares us as a bride adorned for His coming.

---

14. Exodus 14, Joshua 3, 6.

And now, dear children, continue in him, so that when he appears we may be confident and unashamed before him at his coming.

(1 John 2:28)

We've all been told at some point in our lives, "Don't put the cart before the horse." Abraham got things backwards when he tried to help the Lord give him a son. He created a lot of trouble for himself and Sarah.[15] King Saul put things in reverse order when he acted against Samuel's instructions and offered a sacrifice on his own before going into battle.[16] He lost his kingdom as a consequence. It's an easy mistake because our human nature demands to be in charge and doesn't like waiting for God to act on our behalf.

Instead of charging into battle on our own, we're instructed to wait in the presence of the Lord. This isn't a wait-in-line at the Post Office kind of waiting. It's the "wait" of a bride who is filled with active expectation. It's more than just waiting for the Lord to do something. Instead, the Hebrew word for wait has connotations of "in" the Lord. It means to be bound to Him and to stick close to Him.[17] This Hebrew word offers a vivid picture of being woven together like braiding strands of a rope. In waiting we are like a thin thread being interwoven into a strong, three-stranded cord with the Father, Son, and Holy Spirit.

So instead of getting ahead of God—wait. Remain bound together, or interwoven into the Lord. This is a union that brings us into the power of His holy presence.

Anyone who runs ahead and does not continue in the teaching of Christ does not have God; whoever continues in the teaching has both the Father and the Son.

(2 John 9)

This study concludes by refocusing on the chapter's key Scripture where the Apostle John teaches us about waiting. We learned that it's better to wait "in" the Lord because He holds us closer than a touch. Now we find strength, comfort, and unity as we come together in Jesus' name to wait and pray. The Church began in a gathering of Jesus' disciples who were waiting in prayerful harmony. We must continue meeting in prayerful agreement that strengthens and unites us so that we may carry on the work of the Great Commission. "Together" is a key word here because in the kingdom of heaven there are no mavericks or loose cannons.

---

15. Genesis 16:1-5.
16. 1 Samuel 13:8-14.
17. Hosea 12:6. Hebrew: קָוָה qâvâh.

We examine ourselves as we prepare to assemble, knowing there is cleansing. We don't compare ourselves to others. Instead, we use the Word of God as our standard of measure. With contrite hearts we come together prayerfully to wait in the Lord. In Him we are strengthened to produce good fruit—the fruit of the Vine who is Christ Jesus. We are strengthened to press on in our faith and overcome our fatal imperfections. In prayerful waiting we are united as one with other people of faith so that nothing "will be able to separate us from the love of God that is in Christ Jesus our Lord."[18]

We wait on the Lord, knowing we are feeble vessels. We joyfully exalt our Lord God whose power is best manifested in weakness. And we offer ourselves to serve for His honor and glory.[19] Even though we are feeble, when we stand together united in Christ, we rise up victorious in His strength to press on through every challenge. Even when troubles come like a triple threat, we stand strong as one in Christ. For those who wait in the Lord, even the smallest stone in our pocket can slay the giants that come against us. This is the victory of the bride who waits for her promised Bridegroom.

---

18. Romans 8:38–39.
19. 2 Corinthians 12:9.

Chapter 13

Overcomers in Christ

Q & A

1. How difficult is it to produce good fruit in God's vineyard?

2. Is it possible to live up to a standard of perfection and live a sinless life like Jesus?

3. How is it possible that God's promise to Isaac's son Jacob still covers us today?

4. Why is it impossible for mortal beings to accomplish an eternally effective work on their own?

My Journal Notes:

Assurance in Christ

Key Scripture:

- "Therefore, if anyone is in Christ, he is a new creation. The old has passed away; behold, the new has come." (2 Corinthians 5:17 ESV)

Our heavenly Father's promises are unfailing, surer than sunrise and sunset. Similarly, there is no wavering in the Apostle Paul's bold letter to the Corinthian Church. He leaves no room for doubt that those who are in Christ are made new creations. This is not just a cosmetic cover-up, the latest clothes, or a new hairstyle and makeover. All the old stuff from our past is forgiven and put behind us. We are made spotless—cleaner than fresh fallen snow. We are washed in the blood of the Lamb from the inside out. In this study we'll come to see the evidence in our own lives that confirms the reality of Christ in us and its effect on our lives. Strong evidence of the Spirit of Christ who is at work in us and through us gives us a confident assurance. We used to walk on a broad easy road; but no longer. Now we can walk with confident assurance because we have God's Word to light our pathway.

> Study Prayer:
>
> *Our Father in heaven, your hands made us and formed us; give us understanding to learn your commands.*
>
> A prayer according to Psalm 119:73

Wake up, pull the shades back and throw open your windows to let the morning breeze fill the house with aromas from the fruit of the vine. You know you are living in a vineyard when you can breathe in the sweet fragrance of a bountiful ripe harvest. The blood of the grape[1] in your cup confirms that you are a true worker in God's plentiful harvest.

---

1. Deuteronomy 32:14.

In the same way, you know you are in Christ when you breathe in the pleasing aromas of His bountiful garden.[2] The wind of the Spirit of Yeshua, our Savior, is breathed into you, and by this you know you are children who abide in God Almighty. A simple smell test can confirm that you remain in Christ. You know you are abiding in Him when you are like a breath of fresh air in a fellowship of believers.[3]

> *This is how we know that we live in him and he in us: He has given us of his Spirit.*

(1 John 4:13)

Submitting to an unfamiliar authority figure can stress a person to the breaking point. After an officer of the law detains a person, trust is key to everyone's safety. The motto "trust no one" leads to chaos. But everything is cool when the neighborhood cop approaches us because he's the same guy who waited with us at our bus stop when we were too little to defend ourselves. We know we're safe with him because we trust him and care about him as a friend.

It's much the same for those who are in Christ. We trust Him because we know Him. He's forgiven us and we can approach Him with our burden of guilt washed away. He's the Good Shepherd who holds us close. We've learned to love Him with all our heart. The bond of fellowship is genuine and strong. We know we are in Christ when we trust Him enough to submit to His authority. Those who abide in Him delight in submitting to Him and obeying Him. We learn that it's a joy to do what He teaches.

> *Let us draw near to God with a sincere heart and with the full assurance that faith brings, having our hearts sprinkled to cleanse us from a guilty conscience and having our bodies washed with pure water.*

(Hebrews 10:22)

We deposit our savings in a bank that we trust to keep it for a rainy day. Our retirement account gets invested through a company we're sure will return it to us after we hang up our hard hat for the last time. We pay a building contractor a big chunk of money even before they start the job because we trust them to build our new house. Generous people donate to charities they trust to do the good work they claim they'll do. It also takes a lot of trust for a free economy to function efficiently.

As Jesus' disciples we press forward in the work of the Great Commission even when we suffer because of it. We drive on to do the work of the kingdom

---

2. Song of Songs 4:16.
3. 2 Timothy 1:16.

through hardship and persecution because we are confident of our calling and we trust that He will bring us safely to the end. We can trust the Almighty, knowing our faithfulness in little things serves as an integral part in a greater work.[4] We can start each task with a confident hope, knowing that the Lord God is faithful to bring us to our reward on the day our Savior returns to take us home.

> *That is why I am suffering as I am. Yet this is no cause for shame, because I know whom I have believed, and am convinced that he is able to guard what I have entrusted to him until that day.*

(2 Timothy 1:12)

You're already making plans for how you'll use your extra pay as you walk out of the boss's office. You feel elated. She gave you an excellent work review, offering accolades for a job well done. She commended you for always getting to work on time and sticking to assigned tasks until finished. Then she promised you a generous pay raise. But your next paycheck was the same as before, and there was no extra pay for months after. Your boss was all promise with no produce.

By contrast, the Gospel of Jesus Christ is more than words. The Good news is far greater than telling Bible stories in Sunday School. The message of the cross is powerfully effective to change a child's life and eternal destiny. For children who hear the word and come to saving faith, eternity begins "today."[5]

John the Baptist proclaimed: "Repent, for the kingdom of heaven has come near."[6] Jesus sent out His disciples telling them: "As you go proclaim this message: 'The kingdom of heaven has come near.'"[7] As Jesus walked among the people, He taught them: "The kingdom of heaven is within you."[8] The kingdom is actively at work in all the Father's sons and daughters right now. Jesus healed the sick and raised the dead because life and health are the reality of God's kingdom.[9] He has not changed. By the great promises of the Word and the guarantee of the Holy Spirit who indwells us, we know that our Redeemer lives and is actively present with us today. We are confident in the Gospel message that actively works among us by the power of Christ's presence that affects us every day of our lives. We're assured of a great "paycheck" when we reach our eternal destiny.[10]

---

4. Luke 16:10.
5. 2 Corinthians 6:2.
6. Matthew 3:2.
7. Matthew 10:7.
8. Luke 17:21 NKJV.
9. Proverbs 4:22.
10. Colossians 2:2–3.

> *For we know, brothers and sisters loved by God, that he has chosen you, because our gospel came to you not simply with words but also with power, with the Holy Spirit and deep conviction. You know how we lived among you for your sake.*

(1 Thessalonians 1:4-5)

Treasure hunters spend countless years learning all they can about the Lost Dutchman's Mine in Arizona. They search diligently for the smallest clue that others may have overlooked. Every year hundreds of people pack up and go in search of this mysterious gold mine. Some go it alone and a few have died trying. When speculators find their own secret location, they carefully examine every rock and pebble looking for clues to this vast gold reserve.

But the legendary gold in the elusive Dutchman's Mine is pocket change compared to all the treasure in the kingdom of heaven. We have a kingdom whose riches are a great mystery worth searching out. The best way to find this treasure is in a gathering with people of like faith who work together digging for clues in the Scriptures. Preaching, teaching, and interactive Bible studies all serve to reveal the mystery of Christ. As we grow in grace and the knowledge of Christ, He is revealed in all His glory and splendor. All those who seek the treasures of wisdom and knowledge will surely find it.[11]

> *My goal is that they may be encouraged in heart and united in love, so that they may have the full riches of complete understanding, in order that they may know the mystery of God, namely, Christ, in whom are hidden all the treasures of wisdom and knowledge.*

(Colossians 2:2–3)

When you read the directions for assembling that new gadget delivered to your front door, it soon becomes clear the instructions were poorly translated from a strange language. The squiggly Oriental words make more sense than the backwards English. But little Jimmy is so anxious to have fun with his new remote-control robot that you press on through trial and error, putting the pieces together until you get it right.

Messages of the Old Testament prophets like David the psalmist, Solomon's songs, and all the prophets leading up to John the Baptizer offer an abundance of evidence. Jesus' teaching, the Gospel writers, and the Apostle's letters offer many clues to the mysteries of God's kingdom. Unlike trying to read a strange language, when we start putting the clues together, their messages become as wonderfully simple as a preschool puzzle.

---

11. Matthew 7:7.

When you hear the knock on your heart's door and open to Jesus who is the Way, the Truth, and the Life, the seed of the faith takes root in your heart. It's as simple as "believe and be baptized."[12] As the seed of truth takes root, you realize this simple Good News has a powerful effect on your everyday life. You find yourself delighting to obey His command to believe and love. Your obedient love is the evidence of Christ's indwelling presence and proof that you abide in Him.[13]

> *And this is his command: to believe in the name of his Son, Jesus Christ, and to love one another as he commanded us. The one who keeps God's commands lives in him, and he in them. And this is how we know that he lives in us: We know it by the Spirit he gave us.*

(1 John 3:23–24)

You feel beads of sweat on your forehead as the glaring light blinds you.

"Where were you on January 10th at 3:30 am?"

The detective crosses his arms and leans forward on the table as you try to blink away the glare of the light bulb and the officer's glowering stare. He has the proof in his hands. There are witnesses who collaborate his evidence, and he's confident their testimony will stand up in a court of law. Your mind scrambles to think of anything in your favor.

How can you be confident that you remain in Christ; held safe until judgment day? How can you answer accusers who question your faith? Surely there is some solid evidence of the Spirit of Christ who indwells His people. The Apostle Paul teaches us to examine ourselves to be sure we remain in the faith, but what clues can we offer as proof? The answer is simple. Delighting in obedience, following Jesus' teaching, and applying His words to your everyday life is proof positive that you abide in Christ. What comes out of your mouth reveals who dwells in your heart.[14] This is more than flexing your willpower to make yourself obey the command against cursing or lying.[15] Instead, your obedience is compelled by love for your Lord and Savior who has forgiven and redeemed you.

> *We know that we have come to know him if we keep his commands. Whoever says, "I know him," but does not do what he commands is a liar, and the truth is not in that person. But if anyone obeys his word, love for God is truly made complete in them. This is how we know we are in him.*

(1 John 2:3–5)

---

12. Mark 16:16.
13. 1 John 4:12.
14. Mark 7:20–22, Luke 6:45.
15. Leviticus 19:11.

Remember the evenings you sat on a mossy log with your friends around a campfire, singing, "They'll know we are Christians by our love."[16] The words of John's Gospel inspired the song writer to sing this great chorus.[17] The love of Christ in us is the assurance that we abide in Christ. It's like living where grape vines grow on the hillsides. In the morning when you wake up, you know you live in a château because of the fragrance carried by the breeze. Indeed, the love of Christ at work in us produces a sweet fragrance as evidence of His holy presence.

You know Jesus is ever present because you are forgiven, cleansed, and then restored to sweet fellowship in the Spirit. In the confidence of His presence you minister, serve, and worship with your whole heart and soul. The caring hand you extend and the loving words you speak add to your account in heaven. Your trust grows, knowing a great treasure awaits you in glory. Even when you suffer for the cause of Christ and the cross, you can stand firm in the assurance of your faith.

As you search out the mysteries of the Gospel, you come to see that it's like putting together pieces of a simple puzzle. You learn that the Good News is so much more than words on a page in a book. It's like a treasure you can hold out in your hands. It's like fragrant words to speak out with your mouth. When the picture puzzle comes together, you see that you have a reason for confident assurance. It becomes evident in every word you speak and everything you set your hands to do.

Start searching for pieces of the puzzle today. "Press on toward the goal to win the prize."[18] The words of the holy Scriptures open the mysteries of the Gospel and the kingdom of heaven so that you may press on with a confident assurance, knowing that the Spirit of Christ Jesus dwells in you. He will hold you close until He returns for you. Our heavenly Father keeps in trust all that you have committed to Him as your treasures in heaven.

> *That is why I am suffering as I am. Yet this is no cause for shame, because I know whom I have believed, and am convinced that he is able to guard what I have entrusted to him until that day.*
>
> (2 Timothy 1:12)

---

16. "They'll Know We Are Christians," hymn by Peter Scholtes, F.E.L. Publications, 1966.
17. John 13:35.
18. Philippians 3:14.

Chapter 14

Assurance in Christ

Q & A

1. What is the evidence of Christ Jesus' indwelling presence, and what clues show that we abide in Him?

2. When does eternity begin for those who come to saving faith?

3. What did Jesus mean when He said, "The kingdom of heaven is within you"?

4. Describe the effects of the fragrance of Christ's indwelling presence in you.

My Journal Notes:

Double Portions

Key Scriptures:

- "Instead of your shame you will receive a double portion, and instead of disgrace you will rejoice in your inheritance. And so you will inherit a double portion in your land, and everlasting joy will be yours." (Isaiah 61:7)

- "Return to your fortress, you prisoners of hope; even now I announce that I will restore twice as much to you." (Zechariah 9:12)

This study is a call to double down on our fellowship in Christ. Devoting our lives to serve in the kingdom leads us to effective servanthood. This devotion is powerful because it's two-fold. By grace, through faith Christ indwells us and by faith we enter into the fullness of Christ. This union is like double teaming against the evil desires of our past that still tempt us.[1]

Levitical law required that a father's firstborn son receive a double portion of his property as an inheritance. This foreshadows the Son of God, the firstborn of Creation who came to walk among us as Immanuel. He is also the firstborn of all those who will be raised from the dead. In context, this study's key Scriptures proclaim our heavenly Father's promise of a better covenant.[2] This restoration is ours in the year of the Lord's favor, and is offered to us through Yeshua HaMashiach, who is Christ, our Lord and Savior. He is the victorious second Adam, the double portion of our inheritance, and the one and only Son of Creator God.

The Messiah's final triumphant Jubilee was foreshadowed every fiftieth year as required by Israel's covenant.[3] In Old Testament times this special season came at the end of seven cycles of Sabbatical years. During Jubilee, slaves and prisoners were set free, all debts forgiven, and all land returned to a family according to their portion in the Promised Land as allotted by Joshua.

---
1. James 1:14.
2. Hebrews 8:6.
3. Leviticus 25:8–54.

The following study Scriptures call us to return where we may dwell in the shelter of the Most High, rest in the shadow of the Almighty, and find refuge in His safe fortress.[4] This study directs our attention to the prophet Isaiah's powerful and prophetic chapter sixty-one that proclaims the Jubilee we now have in Christ Jesus every day of our lives and for all eternity. Then Elisha concludes our study with a bold request for a double portion upon Elijah's departure in a chariot of fire.

> Study Prayer:
>
> *Our Father, teach us your ways so we may know you and continue to find favor with you.*
>
> A prayer according to Exodus 33:13

Isaiah prophesied the fulfillment of Christ's Jubilee. He looked forward to see the day when Jesus would unroll the scroll in Nazareth's synagogue to read from the prophet's words and then proclaim Isaiah's prophecy fulfilled.[5] By faith we are blood-bought sons and daughters of our heavenly Father; set free in Christ's Jubilee. By hearing and believing the Word, the chains of sin are broken. We die with Christ in holy baptism and then death loses its grip on us. Doors of the prison that hold us swing open to release us. In the light of the Word and the fire of the Spirit we are brought out of the world's darkness.

Christ inhabits the redeemed with His holy presence. Because of this we are called to serve as cleansed temples where He may dwell. We can only live this submitted life by the power of God's word. The Word strengthens us to resist yearnings that cause our hands to reach out for what is not ours. The holy Scriptures help us to resist the temptation to feast our eyes on delights of the flesh. Meditating on the Word empowers us to stop entertaining our sinful thoughts.[6] The Bible's imperatives lead us to abide in Christ in faithfulness and in accord with His indwelling presence. We are called to serve as blood-bought bond servants.[7] Chains that once bound us are broken. Instead of exalting our flesh we make sure it remains dead to sin. When the prison doors are thrown open, we make a fast exit and leave all depravity behind. With the Holy Scriptures as our light, we walk a narrow, well-lit path. In His presence we delight to be obedient to the Apostles instructions in their letters to the churches.

This is true freedom in Christ.

---

4. Psalm 91:1–2.
5. Luke 4:21.
6. This truth was foreshadowed in Yehovah's command to observe the Passover feast in Exodus 13:9.
7. 1 Corinthians 7:22 ESV.

The Spirit of the Sovereign Lord is on me, because the Lord has anointed me to proclaim good news to the poor. He has sent me to bind up the brokenhearted, to proclaim freedom for the captives and release from darkness for the prisoners.

(Isaiah 61:1)

This fallen world is tangled in the tentacles of misery, holding many people in its vicious grip. Young people despair of life and want to check out. They're a generation living without a foundation to build their lives on. We've hidden away the light that could show our children the right pathway.[8] The world's hostility surrounds our sons and daughters, fears assault at every turn and they wander aimlessly without direction.

Rise up, O Christian, and proclaim the Lord's Jubilee; the year of His favor, and show the way for those who grieve in despair. Open the holy Scriptures so that lost souls will hear, receive, and believe. God's word lights the way for all who will come to Christ, who is the way, the truth, and the life.[9] Our Savior leads wandering souls into the light and then wraps them in His righteousness. The Good Shepherd then presents all redeemed sons and daughters before His heavenly Father. Those who come to saving faith are given a new name and an eternal promise. They are pledged as a bride. In the light of Christ, they live in the Father's presence saturated in beautiful fragrances of joy and gladness. Indeed, we bring wandering souls to Christ in their mournful rags and they are clothed with robes of righteousness, praise, and thanksgiving.

To proclaim the year of the Lord's favor and the day of vengeance of our God, to comfort all who mourn, and provide for those who grieve in Zion–to bestow on them a crown of beauty instead of ashes, the oil of joy instead of mourning, and a garment of praise instead of a spirit of despair. They will be called oaks of righteousness, a planting of the Lord for the display of his splendor.

(Isaiah 61:2–3)

An entire generation of Americans has fallen into a pit of despair.[10] How could this happen right before our eyes? The Almighty established a strong foundation for our nation, but today leaders of every persuasion chip away at this groundwork with lies and deceit. Our forefathers opened their deliberations with prayers to God who governs the affairs of men. But today our representatives pray to whoever pleases them. The core of our society has no Rock in whom our children can anchor their lives. So many of our neighbors

---

8. Matthew 5:15.
9. Chapter 24 in the Author's book, The Greatest Love, provides a Scriptural path to lead someone to Christ.
10. Lauren Gaydosh et al., "The Depths of Despair Among US Adults Entering Midlife," American Journal of Public Health 109, no. 5 (May 1, 2019): 774-780, https://doi.org/10.2105/AJPH.2019.305002.

and co-workers live hopeless lives. The fabric of our nation unravels before our eyes. But do we just look on and say; "Oh well, what can I do?"

"They" in this section's verse speaks to all those who are captives of hope. Christ Jesus strengthens us to help rebuild crumbling families. There is so much at stake. Whole communities are collapsing into decay. The beautiful and spacious skies and amber waves of grain turn to rust and dust. The fruited plain has eroded into a valley of grieving tears. Our once alabaster cities are stained with the blood of violence at every turn. We turned halls of justice into chambers of injustice. Because we have defiled the earth with our sin, a land once blessed with abundance is now riven with dry desert wastelands. Our joy has turned to mournful weeping.

But we are captives of a great hope. Jesus' followers are beckoned to make the ruins of this nation into a place where the blessings of heaven's rain can shower down to create pools that refresh us.[11] In Christ we are called and anointed to make the divisive States of America united again. This good work begins with earnest prayer. In Christ we are empowered to rebuild a nation united in hope. Our first job is to bend our knees, then roll up our sleeves, put on our gloves, and pick up the ruined bricks and stones of ruined lives and restore the promise of Jesus' holy name.

The renewal begins with Christians praying like Daniel to repent of the sins of a nation.[12] Restoration takes root in contrite hearts. We are called to grieve over the sin that surrounds us and lift up Christ who restores. Strap on truth like a tool belt, put on the helmet of salvation like a hard hat, plug your tools into the power source, and begin the good work of restoring people and rebuilding lives out of the rubble and ruins.

> *They will rebuild the ancient ruins and restore the places long devastated; they will renew the ruined cities that have been devastated for generations.*

(Isaiah 61:4)

Priests in Israel's Levitical system fulfilled various functions. Some practiced healing arts like a pharmacist, mixing medicinal oils, herbs, and spices. Others served as doormen or guards in the temple. Musicians and singers led the people to shout out with praise and exalt the Lord with worshipful psalms. Many served as judges to settle people's disputes. Some were privileged to work with their hands as temple craftsmen. Some Levites were charged with accounting for the offerings and managing the temple storehouses. A few were blessed to serve at the altars of sacrifice.

---

11. Psalm 84:6.
12. Daniel 9:3-6.

As working parts of the Church we are all anointed to serve before Yeshua our High Priest. No one is left out. All Christians are called to serve as priests in the Church. When the Levitical priests served, they stood in the shadow of the promised Messiah. Today those who work as priests in our gatherings serve in the light of Christ.

Today we are ordained to serve in many different ways, according to our call in Christ.[13] This is an awesome duty because this service is endowed by the Spirit of Christ. Under the Law the Spirit of Messiah stood with the priests and prophets who served. In the Church the Spirit of Christ indwells to empower priests who worship, serve and minister. The Word and the Spirit compel us to enter into the fullness of Christ's holy presence as we serve. He is our double portion and in Him we serve in one accord as working parts of the whole Church.

And you will be called priests of the Lord, you will be named ministers of our God. You will feed on the wealth of nations, and in their riches you will boast.

(Isaiah 61:6)

A heart that delights in the Lord is a treasure worth more than all the silver and gold locked in all the nation's vaults and hidden in the earth. Souls that rejoice in the God of our salvation are more precious than the treasures of every nation. Consider the condition of our lives before we were called to Christ and to repent of our sin before the Throne of Grace.[14] Sin brought us down to the dregs of life. Then our hearts broke when we saw our sinfulness and our need of Christ. We came with nothing to offer but filthy rags. We were spiritual paupers with a death sentence hanging over our heads.

But in a moment of the Lord's favor, He lifted us up from the pit of darkness. He gave us repentant hearts that grieve over our sin and sinfulness. He washed us in His shed blood to make us clean. Because He is faithful and just, our Lord Jesus forgives us our sins and cleanses us of every stain. Then He gives us good gifts, anointing us as a bride adorned with precious stones and jewels. In unity of the bride and Bridegroom, High Priest and servant priests, we all work together in agreement to double team the forces of darkness. Together we build on the foundation Rock, who is Yeshua, our Lord and Savior.[15]

---

13. Note author's book: Treasures of the Kingdom, chapter 7, Kingdom Treasures in Spiritual Gifts.
14. Haggai 2:15.
15. Haggai 2:18-23.

> *I delight greatly in the Lord; my soul rejoices in my God. For he has clothed me with garments of salvation and arrayed me in a robe of his righteousness, as a bridegroom adorns his head like a priest, and as a bride adorns herself with her jewels.*

(Isaiah 61:10)

Be bold in the cause of the Great Commission. Be confident in your assigned task.[16] Be fearless in your calling as a priest in God's kingdom and then press in and take up the sword of the Spirit. Rise up as a mighty army to work in His harvest field. Christ is power and strength in us and in Him we are made ready and willing on His day of battle. We are doubly strong when our everyday battles are fought in the power and strength of Christ victorious.

We armor up to serve Almighty God who is King above all kings and Lord above all lords. We join in with God who is mighty in battle. We come wrapped in the righteousness of Jesus Christ. Our hands are washed clean and our hearts made pure. In Christ who has redeemed us, we come blameless before our heavenly Father. We seek Him with all our heart and soul, and then live in agreement with our Savior who indwells us. As we ascend to Mount Zion the gates swing open. With bold hearts we enter into the presence of the King of glory who receives us with great celebration. This twofold victory is ours because we abide in Christ who indwells us.

> *When they had crossed, Elijah said to Elisha, "Tell me, what can I do for you before I am taken from you?" "Let me inherit a double portion of your spirit," Elisha replied.*
> *"You have asked a difficult thing," Elijah said.*

(2 Kings 2:9–10)

How does a redeemed soul come into a double portion of Christ; the double inheritance of the firstborn? In ancient cultures the firstborn son was known as the first fruits of a father's strength. Because of this the eldest received a double inheritance.[17] We see this principle fulfilled in Christ who is our portion. We enter into Christ who is the first fruits of resurrection power. By the power of the cross and Jesus' shed blood we are made one in Christ. We are called to remain in Christ who is our portion. It may help to look at it like a mathematical equation: Christ in us + Us in Christ = A double portion, a double blessing, and a double inheritance. Remember that abiding in Christ does not happen magically. The words we speak on our own can't make it happen. This powerful union is the work-out-our-salvation part of a walk of faith.[18] This means we allow the Word to work in us every morning, noontime, evening, and nighttime.

---

16. Mark 13:34.
17. Deuteronomy 21:17.
18. Philippians 2:12.

In Christ we enter into His Jubilee year of favor where we find freedom to live to the full every day of our lives. We're empowered to speak out what we hear our Lord Jesus speaking. Indeed, we're anointed by the Spirit of Christ to proclaim freedom to the prisoner. But in freedom Jesus' good work has just begun. We serve as priests who prayerfully help to restore ruined lives by enlightening their hearts with the Word, and leading them to Christ who heals body, soul, mind, and spirit. Our sin has defiled the earth and brought us to ruin. But we are raised up like a mighty army to rebuild our cities streets with peaceful dwellings.

Those who abide in Christ and rise up with zeal are like Elisha who asked for a powerful double portion. This is only possible in Christ the only Son of God who is the first fruits of resurrection power.

Chapter 15

Double Portions

Q & A

1. How do sons and daughters of God Almighty come into a double portion?

___

2. Will you enter into Christ in His two-fold victory?

___

3. What did the Apostle Paul mean when he said: "Work out your salvation with fear and trembling"?

___

4. What blessings are poured out upon God's people when the foundation is prepared in God's holy temple?

___

My Journal Notes:

The Revelation of Yeshua, our Lord and Savior

Key Scriptures:

- "On that day you will realize that I am in my Father, and you are in me, and I am in you." (John 14:20)

- "And this is the testimony: God has given us eternal life, and this life is in his Son. Whoever has the Son has life; whoever does not have the Son of God does not have life." (1 John 5:11–12)

The Bible holds countless pearls of truth and wisdom like treasures stored in golden bowls. When we hear and receive the Word, we are enriched in the kingdom of heaven. We sing out with psalms and hymns to fix these nuggets of truth in our memory. Then we can croon out every day of the week in rhythm with the work of our hands. One beautiful expression of truth in song is: "Christ in me the hope of glory."[1] Many Christians understand and internalize the words of Scripture, but we have to think about what they really mean and how to apply the songs we sing to our daily lives. How can our eyes be opened to see the glory and majesty of Christ who indwells every soul He redeems? Is His indwelling presence only a distant hope or a present reality in everyday life? This chapter's purpose is to encourage Christians to be vigilant in our faith and come into the fullness of Christ.[2]

In this study we'll see greater revelation of the Anointed One, our Lord and Savior. This insight will help us check our vision so we will not slip away in our walk of faith.[3] Our search through the Bible leads us to treasures of the Gospel established by the Word in the beginning of time. Then we'll learn how the Word was made manifest to bring His light into the world.[4]

---

1. This Is My Wonderful Story, hymn by Albert B. Simpson, Tabernacle Hymns #66, 1921.
2. Colossians 2:9-10.
3. Proverbs 29:18.
4. 1 Peter 1:20.

> Study prayer:
>
> *Our soon coming King, may we be wise and listen and learn. Let us discern for guidance, understand proverbs and parables, sayings of the wise, and the mysteries of your wisdom.*
>
> A prayer according to Proverbs 1:5–6

It's our heavenly Father's nature to draw back the clouds of darkness and reveal Himself so that His sons and daughters may see the light and know Him. Does it seem contradictory that the Gospel is hidden from some? If God hides Himself, is it a contradiction of all that is true and right?[5] When the Bible says His glory is invisible, his counsels are unsearchable, and His acts unfathomable, does this contradict His nature? Do Isaiah's prophetic words about a Creator God who shrouds Himself contradict what Paul writes about making the light of the Gospel known?

Like the morning sun piercing the horizon, the Lord's brightness drives away darkness for all whose eyes are opened to the knowledge of God. But the mysteries of the Good News Gospel are hidden from those with calloused and hardened hearts.[6] The Light of the World is veiled, as if by thick, dark clouds that hide the morning sun. Those who love the darkness of night turn their backs to the light of Messiah.[7] However, the glorious riches of salvation's mystery are revealed to those who diligently search.[8] The clouds roll back for our eyes to see the flashing light of our Bridegroom who promised to return for us in all His glory and majesty.

> *To them God has chosen to make known among the Gentiles the glorious riches of this mystery, which is Christ in you, the hope of glory.*

(Colossians 1:27)

Christ Jesus our Savior and Redeemer is the radiant light of the kingdom of heaven. He is the eternal hope for all who come to saving faith. We are baptized into His cross of suffering and His death and resurrection. In the fullness of Christ our hearts rejoice to suffer as a Church for a little while as we complete the work of the Great Commission. Our hearts and hands lift up with praise because we know that every blow against us brings us one step closer to Christ who is revealed in the power of resurrection. Every assault

---

5. Psalm 97:2; Isaiah 45:3,15.
6. Matthew 13:15.
7. John 3:19.
8. Isaiah 55:6.

against the Church enlightens us to us the plight of the ungodly and the joy of the expectant bride for her promised Bridegroom. This is the victory of the Lamb of God who gave His life, His body, and His blood to take away the sins of the world.

> *For my Father's will is that everyone who looks to the Son and believes in him shall have eternal life, and I will raise them up at the last day.*

(John 6:40)

Remember the creepy feeling that came over you when you stepped through a friend's front door and heard a barrage of expletives? Your defenses went up and the angry shouting made you feel awkward and uncomfortable. Then as you joined your host for lunch at the kitchen island your senses revolted with visions of food crawling with invisible bugs and germs. The countertops looked like a bacteria factory, encrusted with dried mac and cheese and other unidentifiable tidbits.

When we visit other people's homes we want to know it's a place where we can be at ease in a safe environment. When our Lord Jesus knocks on our heart's door and then enters our "home," He comes in to dine and converse with us.[9] He forgives us and cleanses us from all unrighteousness. He cleans up our "house." He makes it spotless inside and out so He can dwell there in peace with us. Now that we have come to know our Savior, it's our job to cooperate with Him to keep His dwelling place clean. To do this we must examine ourselves.[10] It may be helpful to ask:

- "Are my heart and soul still clean or have they become cluttered and unkempt?"
- "Is my life continually cleansed by the power of the Word and the Holy Spirit?"
- "Do I, in any way, reject correction and discipline of the Spirit and the Word?"[11]
- "Is the fruit of my life in keeping with repentance?"[12]
- "Do I have the things of God in mind, or the things of men?"[13]

A well-kept "home" is a place where the love and unity of Christ flourishes. Spotless and comfortable abodes are notable. They're like a safe island in a world of clutter and waste. Our lives ought to be like clean and spotless

---

9. Revelation 3:20.
10. 2 Corinthians 13:5.
11. Proverbs 15:32.
12. Matthew 3:8.
13. Mark 8:33.

manors where our Lord Jesus may dwell unashamed.[14] But this cleanness is not just a coat of whitewash on the outside. Jesus' cleansing blood washes both the inside and the outside of the vessel.[15] An upright life in Christ is light to the world, revealing the love of our Savior who shines out to those who are caught in the grips of the world's darkness.

> *I in them and you in me–so that they may be brought to complete unity. Then the world will know that you sent me and have loved them even as you have loved me.*
>
> (John 17:23)

The wisdom of Christ is hidden from people who exalt themselves as wise and intellectual.[16] Considering oneself wise in a worldly way tends to blind one's eyes to the light of heaven's wisdom. When the Wisdom of Creation spoke all things into being, saying, "Let there be light," the chaos of darkness retreated.

The Light of the World is revealed in us and dwells in us so that we will never be overpowered by Satan's evil forces. The gates of the kingdom of darkness will never prevail in their battle to destroy the body of Christ, the Church.[17] In Christ we are armored in light to stand against all principalities and powers of the air. But we must stand as one people, united in Christ, true to Him just as He has revealed Himself. When we are divided from Christ we have no strength to endure.

> *In him was life, and that life was the light of all mankind. The light shines in the darkness, and the darkness has not overcome it.*
>
> (John 1:4–5)

I've never heard of a burglar who sent an announcement to tell when he would come to rob our home. No, he hides himself, lurking in the bushes around his targeted house at dusk. He's an opportunist who may be desperate enough to ravage our home and do away with anyone who stands in his way. He's like a dark shadow that slips in unseen, leaving death and devastation in his wake.

By contrast, Yehovah God enlightened the Old Testament prophets who proclaimed the coming Messiah. With great hope they pointed forward to Immanuel who would come as God with us. The prophets told of Christ, who is the light who dawns upon those who once lived in the shadow of death.[18] The prophets told of an immaculate conception, a newborn child, and a

---

14. 1 John 2:28.
15. Luke 11:39.
16. 1 Corinthians 1:27–29.
17. Matthew 16:17–19.
18. Matthew 4:16.

refugee from Egypt. They looked forward to see their Redeemer and Savior. They stood in the shadow of Christ who is Healer, Teacher, and a just and righteous ruler who would deliver His people from bondage. Their prophetic words point us to Jesus the Christ who indwells us with the fullness of life. The prophet's insights are still proclaimed so that we may live in love that surpasses all knowledge. We are a people of vision, filled with a double portion of all the fullness of our Father in heaven.[19]

> *The thief comes only to steal and kill and destroy; I have come that they may have life, and have it to the full.*

(John 10:10)

The following verse concisely portrays a message about Christ who indwells His followers. When His disciples abide in Him a powerful union is made complete. This dynamic is so great that the world around us is impacted with undeniable bursts of light, like laser beams that reveal our Savior's love.

The uniting power of a union with Christ and the love that flows out to affect the world around us is earth shaking. Jesus' love is more contagious than a viral pandemic. News headlines do not proclaim this love and your news feed ignores it, but the power of His love is never concealed from those who seek Him. Over two thousand years ago, religious stalwarts of the day tried to bury this love, and three days later love burst out of its tomb in the radiant light of resurrection power. Today, we are bound together in a powerful covenant of love. Our part is to be vigilant in our everyday life in agreement with the resurrected Christ who indwells us.

> *I in them and you in me–so that they may be brought to complete unity. Then the world will know that you sent me and have loved them even as you have loved me.*

(John 17:23)

Like building stone upon precious stone, people of Christian faith are united in the fellowship of God's only Son. The love of Christ is the mortar that holds us together. This is not a building we can build on our own. If we attempt to build with our own hands, our labor has no eternal value and the house will crumble. We can work hard, even sacrificing our health and well-being, but if we build according to our own purpose and plan, our sweat will not hold the building together.[20]

The temple dwelling we build is not a lone house out on a prairie. It's a sanctuary with many rooms built together and united by the Spirit of the

---

19. Ephesians 3:19.
20. Ezekiel 44:17–18.

indwelling Christ. A Church united in love and truth is as pleasant as a garden that grows fragrant myrrh and spices. It's a garden as comforting as milk and sweet as honey. This fruitful grove is a place where sons and daughters of vision gather to drink their fill of Christ's love.[21]

> *And in him you too are being built together to become a dwelling in which God lives by his Spirit.*

(Ephesians 2:22)

People of faith who are hungry to hear God's word and compelled by love to do what it says are like the waves of the sea that wash the shorelines of every continent, island, and peninsula on planet Earth. The love of Christ is the catalyst for all who search the Scriptures so they can grow in grace and knowledge and delight in greater vision. This abundant life affects our neighbors and communities. We dig into the mysteries of the Gospel so that we are always prepared to give and answer for the hope we have in Christ.

It's necessary to caution those who become complacent about growing in their faith. Without revelations of truth and a vision for righteousness we become a people without restraint. People run wild without self-control when they refuse to learn from the precepts of the holy Scriptures.[22] Indeed, our Savior is long suffering with us. He is faithful even when we are not faithful.[23] We are spurred on when we consider how few days we have to fulfill our calling in Christ and complete the work of the Great Commission.[24] It's time for God's people to stand up and be vigilant to live in the full revelation of Jesus Christ. We put on the armor of light and grasp hold of heaven's hidden treasures so that we may shine out with the light of Christ that drives back the darkness that surrounds us.

> *My goal is that they may be encouraged in heart and united in love, so that they may have the full riches of complete understanding, in order that they may know the mystery of God, namely, Christ, in whom are hidden all the treasures of wisdom and knowledge.*

(Colossians 2:2–3)

In Christ we have a "one another" walk of faith. Faith is necessary for our salvation, and believing hearts bring us into a sweet fellowship of Jesus' disciples. Too many Christians try to walk alone in Christ, forgetting that by themselves they are like a single-celled amoeba. Christian YouTube channels

---

21. Song of Songs 5:1.
22. Proverbs 29:18.
23. 2 Timothy 2:13.
24. Psalm 90:12.

don't know you, your needs, or your personal conflicts. Television evangelists don't know what you suffer unless you mail in a check with your prayer request. Church at home, alone with our children, doesn't provide all the teaching and correction every Christian needs to grow in grace and knowledge. Church streamed into our home while we're still in our pajamas doesn't provide the opportunities we need to exercise spiritual gifts that build up the body of Christ. Besides all that, virtual church doesn't provide free coffee, doughnuts, and a time to laugh with our friends.

The choruses and hymns we sing as a congregation implant truth in our hearts and minds. The words we sing carry us through our week-day routines. When a worship assembly responsively echoes the words of the Psalms, our hearts are filled with an attitude of gratitude and praise. Hearing the words of Scripture plants seeds of faith to grow in our heart and soul, and then continues to nourish the growing seedlings. Christ Jesus our High Priest is present in our gatherings, revealing Himself as He ministers to the assembly. The ministries of Christ, who is revealed to us, are too awesome to toss aside. Because we serve Christ who is victorious, we are called to be vigilant in our faith and not neglect times of worship in a community of faith.

> *Let the message of Christ dwell among you richly as you teach and admonish one another with all wisdom through psalms, hymns, and songs from the Spirit, singing to God with gratitude in your hearts.*

(Colossians 3:16)

The hand of the Lord lifted Ezekiel up to witness the God of Israel returning to the temple in all His glory. In his vision he saw "a man whose appearance was like bronze"[25] with a measuring rod in his hand. Ezekiel looked on as the temple was measured with meticulous accuracy. It was measured to keep what was holy separate from the common. Then the Lord brought Ezekiel to the gate facing east where he saw the glory of the God of Israel come like a roar of rushing waters in radiant glory. And the glory of the Lord filled the temple.

The man with the measuring rod instructed Ezekiel to show the people plans for the temple so they could envision it as a model for their lives. This is a vital truth because temples where the Lord dwells in all His glory must measure up to the standard. God's word is the measuring rod used to prove that what the Lord established in our lives is kept separate from the common things of this world. This separation keeps us from worshiping and serving created things rather than the Creator. We worship in spirit and truth when we exalt the Creator as He has revealed Himself and by worshiping none other.

---

25. Ezekiel 40:3.

We are measured and found worthy because we abide in Christ. He dwells in temples that are washed and cleansed by the blood of the Lamb. Now we may come boldly before the Father with a clean heart—a heart free of guilt. Our sin-stained lives are washed with water separated to serve a holy purpose.[26] We are cleansed in the blood of the Lamb of God. This is a temple where God comes to dwell in radiant glory.

> *Let us draw near to God with a sincere heart and with the full assurance that faith brings, having our hearts sprinkled to cleanse us from a guilty conscience and having our bodies washed with pure water.*

(Hebrews 10:22)

As we press on to search for pearls of truth and wisdom the mystery of the Gospel that is readily unveiled. Our quest leads us to a narrow gate. The gate swings open so we may enter into the glorious riches of the kingdom of heaven. By grace and through faith we are raised up with Christ in resurrection power—death's grip is broken and we are free in Christ. This is not an easy path because we are called to complete Christ Jesus' suffering in His body, the Church. But we can face our foe, standing as a united Church, a mighty army armored up, ready and willing to do battle.

We are forgiven and cleansed so that Christ may dwell in us. Remember that Jesus referred to His body as a temple. The Apostle Paul taught that our bodies are temples where the Spirit of Christ dwells. Now consider Jesus who walked among us. He was tempted and tested to prove that His temple measured up to God's perfect standard. The measuring of Ezekiel's temple prefigured Jesus' forty days of testing in the wilderness. Overcoming Satan's temptations served to reveal the full measure of Jesus' perfection. We are Christ's redeemed and we are called to live as overcomers. We rise up in the power of resurrection. We stand strong in vigilant faith to live in the fullness of Christ. Our hearts and lives are cleansed so we may serve as a temple where our Advocate and Comforter may dwell in peace.[27]

The Almighty's sons and daughters are joined together in Christ and we must remain united in Him. We are a mighty army called to put on the armor of light and be willing and ready on His day of battle. We are reflections of the light of Christ. We are called to live victorious. Our love of Christ compels us to live our everyday lives in keeping with repentance and in agreement with our Savior who indwells us. By faith we come together as a family. We, the Church, are like many rooms built together, encompassed by a fragrant garden where the wind of the Spirit wafts through the vines in the vineyard.

---

26. Chapter 2 in the author's study guide, Great Separations, provides an in-depth teaching on this topic.
27. John 14:16.

The revelation of the Word renews and strengthens us. This is vital because, without revelation, fallible people run amuck and lose their grasp on the treasures of the kingdom of heaven. We soon learn that it's too difficult to be a part of the body of Christ in isolation. Certainly, we come into many blessings as we pray and worship alone. But remember that our Savior indwells His Church with His mighty presence when we gather in Jesus' holy name to pray in agreement. Let us look to the Temple who is Jesus. He fully measured up to God's standard of perfection, so that He may come like a pent-up flood and fill our temples with His glory.

Chapter 16

The Revelation of Yeshua, our Lord and Savior

Q & A

1. Why is it vital for Christians to live as a people of vision?
   _____
   _____
   _____

2. Describe the temple where our High Priest, Jesus Christ will dwell.
   _____
   _____
   _____
   _____

3. How do we benefit by gathering to worship in a community of faith?
   _____
   _____
   _____
   _____

4. How are the clouds rolled back so that we may see the mystery of Christ and the Gospel?
   _____
   _____
   _____
   _____

My Journal Notes:

Kept Safe to the End

Key Scriptures:

- "We know that we are children of God, and that the whole world is under the control of the evil one. We know also that the Son of God has come and has given us understanding, so that we may know him who is true. And we are in him who is true by being in his Son Jesus Christ. He is the true God and eternal life." (1 John 5:19–20)

- "Yet at present we do not see everything subject to them.[1] But we do see Jesus, who was made lower than the angels for a little while, now crowned with glory and honor because he suffered death, so that by the grace of God he might taste death for everyone." (Hebrews 2:9)

Psalm ninety-one begins with a powerful expression of what it means to be in Christ.[2] Our Redeemer is the shelter of the Most High and in Him we rest in the shadow of the Almighty. This study session shows us the value of safely abiding in Christ, the confident assurance of being clothed with Christ, and the abundant joy of the indwelling Spirit of Christ. The following Scriptures rekindle our understanding of the meaning and significance of these truths—abiding, dwelling, and being clothed with enduring strength that is ours as Christ indwells us.

This lesson's Scriptures teach us regarding protections that are ours as we abide in the shadow of Jesus' wings.[3] We take refuge in God's strong fortress, settle down to rest in the shadow of His wings, and take shelter in God, our fortress. Now we can surely trust the Spirit of Christ to keep all that we have committed to Him until the day He comes back for His bride.

---

1. "Them" refers to all who are called by Christ's holy name.
2. Psalm 91:1–2.
3. Reference the study on wings of Jesus' prayer shawl in the Author's study book, The Greatest Love, Chapter 11.

> **Study Prayer:**
>
> *Lord our shield, assemble your people–men, women and children, and aliens, so we may listen and learn to fear the Lord our God and carefully follow His precepts.*
>
> A prayer according to Deuteronomy 31:12

It's great news when we hear our doctor repeat, "Perfect, perfect, perfect," while reviewing our blood test. But there's a more important blood test than one from a lab.

Our Lord Jesus holds us in the hollow of His hands[4] until the time comes for our Bridegroom to return for us. Then He will present us to the Father who is seated on His throne. Entering before Creator God requires that we pass a blood test. But it's not the blood in mortal veins that is tested. It's the blood of Jesus Christ who makes us, "Perfect, perfect, perfect," in God's sight.

This righteousness is given through faith in Jesus Christ to all who believe. (Romans 3:22)

We have no strength of our own sufficient to help us endure to the end. Every day of our lives as soldiers of the cross we must fight our way through the chaos of a fallen world. The battle is necessary because this deteriorating green-blue orb is not yet placed "under our feet." The Lord strengthens us to fight the battle year after year even in our old age. Many days during the golden years become a test of faith like no other season of our lives. With every birthday our physical strength slips away like sand in an hourglass. But we have an eternal hope.

No Christians of any age can stand alone in their own strength. Our Lord Jesus not only lifts us up and sustains us, He holds us close to His heart. Abiding in Christ strengthens this bond. Who is this Savior who takes up residence in our temple? He came humbly as a servant and was raised up in strength, love, joy, comfort, and the power of resurrection. Consider the elements of His presence that He brings into our lives. His attributes saturate every fiber of our being and then we, in turn, have everything we need to live in agreement with His holy presence,

We rise up in the morning in His strength. We face the challenges of our work day in the might of His presence. The power of Word and the Holy Spirit energizes us to serve our family, church, and community. Joy lights up

---
4. Isaiah 51:16.

our faces even when the cares of this world press in on us. In Christ we are armored up to rise together as a mighty army.

Finally, be strong in the Lord and in his mighty power.

(Ephesians 6:10)

For just a moment, stand at the threshold of eternity and look forward to see that great day when the forces of darkness are finally defeated. The Ancient of Days will confront the wicked at His fiery throne of judgment. The court is seated, the books opened, and every mortal being is called to account even for the careless words they spoke.[5]

As we wait for God's enemies to be defeated we are strengthened in our faith in Jesus Christ so we may live as overcomers. The darkness of sin and its power over us is broken, and we live as sons and daughters protected in a sure and eternal promise. Our confidence comes from knowing the Lord Almighty who dwells in us. He is sovereign and rules over all.[6] Our treasures are stored up in heaven for us where we will receive our just reward.[7]

You, dear children, are from God and have overcome them, because the one who is in you is greater than the one who is in the world.

(1 John 4:4)

Christ in us fortifies us with boldness and confidence. In Him there is safety and protection of a mighty fortress that never fails. This unshakeable bulwark surrounds us to keep safe all that we have committed to Him until the day our Savior returns for us.[8] With the glorious riches of Christ in us, we come to abide in Him where we are saturated in His showers of blessings. These godsends are like entering into a flourishing garden where the Tree of Life blossoms to produce beauty, peace, joy, comfort, and strength. These promises are ours to have and hold because of Yeshua HaMashiach, our coming Messiah. Every attribute of Christ Jesus is ours because we come to Him with repentant hearts, we are forgiven and our temple is cleansed so that He may take up residence in us in all His holiness. Now, in Christ we also abide in the Father. He welcomes us into His rest.

We know also that the Son of God has come and has given us understanding, so that we may know him who is true. And we are in him who is true by being in his Son Jesus Christ. He is the true God and eternal life.

(1 John 5:20)

---

5. Daniel 7:9–10, Matthew 12:36.
6. Psalm 103:19.
7. Psalm 58:11.
8. 2 Timothy 1:12.

When building a house to shelter our growing family we start with a foundation. Then we build on the foundation brick upon brick, using mortar to cement them together. Finally, we'll need to cover our house with a roof to keep out the stormy weather.

As Christians, a sure foundation is provided for us—the Rock who is Christ Jesus.[9] We build on this foundation with love, truth, hope, and promises of the holy Scriptures.[10] Even the mortar is supplied; the power of our Savior's loving kindness.[11] We must do our part to build a strong spiritual house that will endure to the end.[12] Those who abide in Christ keep themselves in God's love and grow in grace and knowledge by constructing a solid house. This is a good work to accomplish as we wait for our Bridegroom to return.

> *But you, dear friends, by building yourselves up in your most holy faith and praying in the Holy Spirit, keep yourselves in God's love as you wait for the mercy of our Lord Jesus Christ to bring you to eternal life.*

(Jude 20–21)

Two people working together can produce three times what one person can do. When you have a work partner, one can pick up the slack if the other has a bad day. If you're picking apples from the top limbs and fall, what will you do if there's no one to help? When you go to bed on a frigid night, how can you keep warm unless you have your spouse to snuggle with you? When confronted with a violent attacker, one might be overpowered, but two can put up a strong defense.[13]

There is power in numbers. We can't stand alone as we endure in our faith. We gain a great confidence in our worshipful assemblies. Jesus Christ serves as our High Priest and He gathers us together in His fold to keep us safe. Together, in Christ, we come into heaven's High and Holy Place, covered by the blood of Christ, confident in our faith, assured we are clean, and free of all guilt and shame. Indeed, the Church is strengthened in the fellowship of Christ and His body. Together we are made strong so we may endure to the end.

---

9. Matthew 7:25.
10. John 17:17.
11. Colossians 1:17.
12. Philippians 2:12.
13. Ecclesiastes 4:9–12.

> *Therefore, brothers and sisters, since we have confidence to enter the Most Holy Place by the blood of Jesus, by a new and living way opened for us through the curtain, that is, his body, and since we have a great priest over the house of God, let us draw near to God with a sincere heart and with the full assurance that faith brings, having our hearts sprinkled to cleanse us from a guilty conscience and having our bodies washed with pure water. Let us hold unswervingly to the hope we profess, for he who promised is faithful. And let us consider how we may spur one another on toward love and good deeds, not giving up meeting together, as some are in the habit of doing, but encouraging one another–and all the more as you see the Day approaching.*

(Hebrews 10:19–25)

How many calories do adults need every day to keep themselves healthy and strong? The answer depends on how active we are. An Olympic athlete requires up to four thousand calories to keep strong. A couch potato only requires a little over fifteen hundred calories per day. Our lifestyle determines our requirement for nutrition.

Those who are spiritually active become strong by consuming more and more of God's word. They become diligent students of the Scriptures. They dig deep into God's word, hear the truth, and then sprint out like athletes to minister and serve according to the power of the Word at work in them. To get strong in the Lord we need empowering nourishment, and that comes by partaking of Christ. Those who run the race to be crowned a winner must go into training.[14] Vigorous preparation makes us hungry and our spirit yearns for more of the Word. The holy Scriptures create a craving for the Lord's Table where we feast upon Christ, the Bread of Life, and partake of the cup—His cleansing blood. At this table of communion, we are strengthened to proclaim Christ Jesus and His vicarious, redemptive death until He returns for us as He promised. The endurance to finish this race is only in Christ who is our strength. We come into His enduring strength as we abide in Him and partake of Him.

> *For I received from the Lord what I also passed on to you: The Lord Jesus, on the night he was betrayed, took bread, and when he had given thanks, he broke it and said, "This is my body, which is for you; do this in remembrance of me." In the same way, after supper he took the cup, saying, "This cup is the new covenant in my blood; do this, whenever you drink it, in remembrance of me." For whenever you eat this bread and drink this cup, you proclaim the Lord's death until he comes.*

(1 Corinthians 11:23–26)

---

14. 1 Corinthians 9:25.

At the end of a long work day, we're exhausted by the pressures of the jungle. By five o'clock on Friday we're ready for a change of pace and some time off. Then when we open the front door at home and plop our work-laden briefcase on the rug, the kids run to gang up on us; "Let's play catch!" Our weary just got wearier.

We may get weary as time marches on and we look with yearning for our Lord's return. The demands of life's jungle can weigh us down. As we press on with the work of the great commission, we need strength that is greater than any mortal capacity. In fact, in our human weakness the demands of kingdom work are impossible. The work of our calling is only possible by the anointing, gifting, and empowering work of the Holy Spirit. All those who are in Christ are strengthened by means of the Word and the Holy Spirit so we may persevere and endure hardships for His glory and honor. We press on in the power of His holy name to complete every good work that our Lord has begun in us.

> *These are the words of him who holds the seven stars in his right hand and walks among the seven golden lampstands. I know your deeds, your hard work and your perseverance. I know that you cannot tolerate wicked people, that you have tested those who claim to be apostles but are not, and have found them false. You have persevered and have endured hardships for my name, and have not grown weary.*

(Revelation 2:1–3)

When faced with a daunting task we might say, "Rome wasn't built in a day." It's also true that Rome didn't crumble into decay in one day. Everything we do happens one step at a time. Whether we're building a business or getting dressed in the morning, we perform the tasks in orderly steps. It doesn't work to promote a business before we have products to sell. Putting on makeup before taking a shower isn't a good plan.

Yahweh, our Lord God, has begun a good work in every one of His sons and daughters. He molds us and shapes us to be useful vessels in His kingdom and then gives us a job to do. He justifies us and then starts the process of sanctifying us. This is a painstaking process that often feels like coarse sandpaper scratching at us. But we glory in it because we know that suffering produces perseverance. Perseverance leads to godly character, and a tried and tested character creates great hope to keep us safe to the end.[15] When we suffer for the cause of Christ, this serves to complete the work of Jesus' sufferings on the cross and strengthens the Church.[16] We are built up in Christ to complete the work given to Jesus' followers to go and make disciples.

---
15. Romans 5:3–5.
16. Colossians 1:24.

In all my prayers for all of you, I always pray with joy because of your partnership in the gospel from the first day until now, being confident of this, that he who began a good work in you will carry it on to completion until the day of Christ Jesus.

(Philippians 1:4–6)

All those who are in Christ abide in truth and righteousness. Because of the constant attacks from the world around us we need assurance that can only come by dwelling in Him. We get battered because everything in this world is not yet subject to Christ. We need a refuge, a safe place in the shelter of the Most High God. The Father's presence is our refuge. We are a temple cleansed by blood of Christ. We're made perfect, wrapped in Jesus' robe of righteousness and made one with the Almighty triune God.

When the Spirit of Christ indwells us and we walk according to the Spirit, we are fortified with a bold confidence as we stand before the Lord of Hosts. He receives us and welcomes us into His rest. Our standing is sure because we have built our lives on a solid foundation that is Christ Jesus, the Rock of our salvation.[17] This unshakeable foundation keeps us safe until the end of time when Christ returns for His own.

Standing alone makes us more vulnerable when temptation comes our way. A community of faith strengthens us to withstand life's assaults. We're always safer and stronger when we stand shoulder to shoulder in fellowship, geared up with the Almighty's armor. Those who fight the good fight need spiritual nourishment to be strong. As we savor the meat of God's word we are strengthened to do the work of the Great Commission. The nourishment of the Scriptures makes us even hungrier and we are compelled to join with the assembly before the Lord's Table where we partake of the Bread of Life and the cup of Jesus' suffering.

We cannot press forward in the work of the kingdom in mortal strength. If we try, we burn out and grow faint. Our failings teach us that this good work can only be accomplished in the power, strength and anointing of the Spirit of Christ. He ordains a work for each of us to accomplish as we wait for His return. We are molded and shaped into useful vessels by the power of the word and the Holy Spirit. Our lives are honed and polished by the Master Builder who makes us strong for the work of the kingdom.

Our lives are built upon the Rock who is Christ Jesus, in whom we are kept safe until He comes "on the clouds of heaven, with power and great glory,"[18] to take us home where He has prepared a place for us to dwell with Him for eternity.

---

17. Psalm 62:2.
18. Matthew 24:30.

Dear children, let us not love with words or speech but with actions and in truth. This is how we know that we belong to the truth and how we set our hearts at rest in his presence.

(1 John 3:18–19)

Chapter 17

Kept Safe to the End

Q & A

1. What elements are brought into our lives by Christ's indwelling presence?

2. What is the effect of our Savior's presence on our everyday lives throughout the years?

3. How do we get the spiritual nourishment we need for doing the work of our calling?

4. Why do we need a community of faith to help us endure to the end?

My Journal Notes:

Cherishing Found Treasure

Throughout this study, The Mystery Which Is Christ in You, we discovered great nuggets of truth as we searched the Scriptures regarding Christ's indwelling presence. Let's review the evidence that leads us to the great riches that are ours as we abide in Christ. Pick up each precious stone of truth we discovered and examine them again one by one. As we do this, we'll come to value these treasures in our heart of hearts.

The first precious stone is a simple and beautiful oneness with our Lord and Savior. In all of His beauty and majesty, Christ indwells us and then calls us to abide in Him. The Lamb of God established His kingdom to reign within us.[1] Now we can live in harmony with the heartbeat of His kingdom. We put aside our man-made limitations and enter into the fullness of Christ. In Him our empty traditions and religious paradigms melt away like dross that's skimmed off when refining precious metals.[2] Now that we're free of our man-made burdens we can run the race and carry the Good News Gospel to the farthest reaches of the earth.[3]

> *The mystery from which true godliness springs is great: He appeared in the flesh, was vindicated by the Spirit, was seen by angels, was preached among the nations, was believed on in the world, was taken up in glory.*
>
> (1 Timothy 3:16)

The next jewel we take in our hand offers relief from a devastating famine, a drought of hearing the word of the Lord.[4] Our hunger for God's word is rarely satisfied in isolation, but rather in a community of fellowship. Together we are armored up to be ready and willing on the day of battle. In worshipful assemblies we are wrapped in His robe of righteousness. In our gatherings we hear the word preached, taught, and ministered to all who will hear and

---

1. Luke 17:21 NKJV.
2. Proverbs 25:4.
3. Matthew 24:14.
4. Amos 8:11.

receive. As we come together in Jesus' name, we learn God's precepts so we may live in agreement with Christ Jesus' holy presence. We enter into a unity of faith, a covenantal bond and relationship with Yeshua and all the body of Christ. Walking in the Word and living in agreement with His indwelling presence armors us, and then fills us with the light of His holy presence.

Restore us to yourself, Lord, that we may return; renew our days as of old.

(Lamentations 5:21)

Next, take up the Gospel truth as a pearl of great price. Examine it carefully to appreciate its incredible value. Cherish this great treasure and gain great confidence, knowing that all of God's promises are "yes" in Jesus Christ who is the Amen.[5] When we dwell in the Amen, we gain assurance in His forgiveness and cleansing. Then we come boldly to the Throne of Grace to present our petitions before the Lord Almighty.

The dynamic power of Alpha, the first Word of creation, set a firm foundation for us to build our lives upon. Yeshua is the Tree of Life and we partake of Him, receiving His saving grace and forgiveness. Jesus is the Bread of Life who indwells us with healing, joy, strength, peace, and comfort; indeed, all that He is. Christ, the Word, is the key of David and He opens the door to the great mystery of the Gospel.

Again, the kingdom of heaven is like a merchant looking for fine pearls. When he found one of great value, he went away and sold everything he had and bought it.

(Matthew 13:45–46)

We've sleuthed out the clues to the mysteries of the Gospel. Now reach out and reexamine another precious stone. Turn it over and over to enjoy the reflections of color and light. This jewel is the power of a community in fellowship. It's no longer a mystery why Christians gather together to be united in Christ. This is so much better than standing alone in our faith. Our Lord Jesus is present with us even in life's darkest and loneliest moments. But our union with Christ is made stronger when we are united in congregation. We need other Christians' strength, support, and prayers to carry us through to the day our Bridegroom returns for His own.

As we gaze into the beauty of this stone, we can see that the world was created with fellowship in mind. When the light comes on, we realize that Christ's love serves like a bonding agent to keep us all together. His love unites us as we come to the Lord's Table as living sacrifices. His righteousness wraps us, and covers us to make us a holy people united in communion.

---

5. Revelation 3:14.

What good fellowship we once enjoyed as we walked together to the house of God.
(Psalm 55:14 NLT)

In our search we've discarded meaningless distractions like slag rocks thrown in a refuse pile. We can't let them weigh us down. They're dark and shiny, but their glitter is deceptive. It doesn't work to have one hand in the slag pile while holding onto heaven's treasures in the other. We cannot serve two masters. When playing around in darkness we take ourselves outside of our Lord's covering. We soon learn that it's not possible to fake it with an all-knowing God. We can't game the system by putting on a false front to impress others when we gather to worship before Jesus Christ our High Priest.[6] Those who attempt to live a double life gradually go the way of least resistance. Their duplicity leads them to ruin. Every willful sin is like the strike of a hammer on the nails in Jesus' hands to crucify Him again and again.[7]

Jesus' teaching makes it exceedingly clear. We cannot follow Him as a disciple and then slip away to dark pursuits in the night. We have to decide: is money, power, and success more important to us, or will we commit our lives to serve in the kingdom of light? When we live our lives in pursuit of earthly treasures alone, our fruitfulness in Christ suffers and we have nothing to offer the owner of the vineyard.[8]

> *Woe to you, teachers of the law and Pharisees, you hypocrites! You are like whitewashed tombs, which look beautiful on the outside but on the inside are full of the bones of the dead and everything unclean. In the same way, on the outside you appear to people as righteous but on the inside you are full of hypocrisy and wickedness.*
> (Matthew 23:27–28)

As we review the clues to this mystery, let's take up another fine cut diamond and consider its various facets. We learned that we are the Church, the bride of Christ who is preparing herself for the Bridegroom's coming. We must be dressed and ready at every moment of the day and night for His return. We are instructed to stay awake as we wait with joyful expectation. We don't have the vitality that's needed to wait, but we are strengthened as we bind ourselves to the Lord. Our life is like a fragile thread braided together with the Father, Son, and Holy Spirit to make a strong cord that cannot be broken. In His strength we endure to the end, waiting in His holy presence. We find encouragement for our bridal expectations in the sweet fellowship of our gatherings for worship. Our eyes look with longing, and our ears are

---
6. 2 Corinthians 6:16.
7. Hebrews 6:4–6.
8. Mark 12:1–9.

pressed to hear the shout of the watchman: "Look, the bridegroom is coming! Come out and meet him!"

Christ Jesus our Lord and Savior indwells us in the fullness of His presence. Every attribute of His holy presence inhabits us. We are God's called and chosen sons and daughters who bear His name and we must live our lives honoring the name He gave us. Abiding in our Lord and Savior means that our career, life, service, worship, and ministry are all accomplished in agreement with all of who Christ is as He indwells us. In this union of fellowship there is great strength and safety as the Church watches and prepares for His return.

> *Because you have made the Lord your dwelling place–the Most High, who is my refuge–no evil shall be allowed to befall you, no plague come near your tent.*

(Psalm 91:9–10 ESV)

Let us come together to delight in obedience as we abide in Christ. Rise up and gather as His Church where there is forgiveness, cleansing, and healing for the wounds of His people. Let us be pure and holy sanctuaries where our Lord and God may dwell in all the richness of His holy presence.

> *"He himself bore our sins" in his body on the cross, so that we might die to sins and live for righteousness; "by his wounds you have been healed."*

(1 Peter 2:24)

Acknowledgments

A friend recently asked if I would write more study books. His question stirred me to reflect; could I even stop writing? God's word is a fire kindled in my bones. The Word burns in my heart and soul with a message to teach God's people. I cannot keep it in.

The message in this study book confronted me with an impossible task but its writing became possible by the power of the Word and the anointing, gifting, and empowering work of the Holy Spirit. The Spirit and the Word instructed my heart in the night and woke my ears every morning, preparing me to hear the Spirit's teaching. What is written here are words each learner must test by measuring them with God's word as the standard. I'm truly blessed in the work of God's kingdom.

I'm grateful for my loving wife, Susie, who encourages me in more ways than she can imagine. I'm thankful for faithful friends who strengthen me in the faith.

We serve an awesome God who is more than able to complete every good work He begins in His people.